THE ESSENTIAL BOOK

DISCOVERING PERU

TEXT AND PHOTOS:
JOSÉ MIGUEL HELFER ARGUEDAS

EDICIONES DEL HIPOCAMPO S.A.C.

THE ESSENTIAL BOOK

DISCOVERING PERU

N° DE REGISTRO DE PROYECTO EDITORIAL: 3150115050004

1ST EDITION, JULY 2002

2ND. REPRINTING, FEBRUARY 2005

TEXT AND PHOTOS:

José Miguel Helfer Arguedas

AUTHORS AND EDITORS:

Aneta Dukszto and José Miguel Helfer Arguedas

TRANSLATION:

Patricia Cockburn de Cassidy

GRAPHIC DESIGN:

Mario Quiroz Martinez

ILLUSTRATIONS:

Leontina Monzón Brañes and Mario Quiroz Martinez

CARTOGRAPHY:

Grupo Geo Graphos S.R.L.

PRE PRESS:

CECOSAMI S.A.

PRINTING:

Quebecor World Perú S.A.

Hecho el Depósito Legal en la Biblioteca Nacional del Perú:1501032005-0135

ISBN:9972-894-07-X

The photos of the Sipan ear ornaments and the erotic ceramic from page 21 have
been provided by the Rafael Larco Herrera Museum.
The pre-Columbian pieces of art published in this book belong to the Museum of the
Nation, the National Museum of Anthropology, Archaeology and History, the
Bruning Museum, the Rafael Larco Herrera Museum and to private collections.

EDICIONES DEL HIPOCAMPO S.A.C.

Av. Luis Aldana 227 - Lima 13

Copies: 10,000

Telefax (51-1) 4762856   Email: editor@hipocampo.com.pe

PRINTED IN PERU.

www.hipocampo.com.pe

We, the authors of this book, would like to express our thanks to Vilma Arguedas Olivera and Lucyna Dukszto for their constant backing and support for the
realisation of this and all preceding editorial projects of this company. We also want to thank all those who have contributed to this project, as Alberto Arevalo,
Cecilia La Fuente, Roberto Gheller, Remko Dalkmann and many others who have aided us in different ways.

Irregular Peruvian geography. North-eastern Amazon Andes (department of Amazonas).

Peru is the biggest country in South America, after Brazil and Argentina, with a territory of 1,285,216 km². It is located in the central-occidental part of the sub-continent along the Pacific Ocean coast, at a west longitude of between 81° 19' 35" and 68° 30' 11" and a south latitude from 0° 01' 48" to 18° 21' 05".

The Andes Mountain Range crosses the country from North to South forming diverse geographic regions and various altitudes of different climates, generating 84 life zones, of the 115 that exist in the planet.

A rather generic geographic division separates the country into three regions: the arid coastal strip, the irregular mountain range sprinkled with small sierra valleys and the Amazon basin or the jungle.

Nevertheless, since 1941 the Pan-American Geography and History Institute recognises eight geographical regions in Peru: *chala* or coastal strip of up 500 m.a.s.l.; *yunga*, that comprises the valleys and ravines located between 500 and 2300 m in the western basin (maritime *yunga*) and between the 1000 and 2300 m in the eastern basin (fluvial *yunga*); *quechua*, between 2300 and 3500 m, in both of the mountains basins; *jalca* or *suni*, between 3500 and 4100 m; *puna*, between 4100 and 4800 m, (ideal heights for the South American animals of the camel family: llamas, alpacas, vicunas and guanacos and habitat of the majestic condor); *janca*, over 4800 m; *rupa rupa* or high jungle, located on the eastern basic of the Andean mountain range, at 1000 and 400 m; and lastly, *omagua* or low jungle region, the true Amazon region, of an altitude between 400 and 80 m.

Peru borders are, to the north, Ecuador (1529 km); to the north-east, Colombia (1506 km); to the east, Brazil (2822 km); to the south-east, Bolivia (1047 km); and to the south, Chile (169 km). The Peruvian coast is 3080 km long.

The country is divided into 24 departments and one Constitutional Province, Callao. The departments are divided into provinces (194 in the whole country), which are also divided into districts (1,828).

POPULATION

According to the year 2002 figures, Peruvian population reached 26,550 million with an annual growth rate of 1.75%. 50.4% of the population are women and 72.3% live in urban zones, 80% speaks Spanish and the remaining

20% speaks Quechua, Aimara and other Amazon native tongues. 62.7% of the inhabitants live below the poverty line and 15.6 % of the latter face a situation of extreme poverty. The average family income is $1,200 a year, placing the country at a medium-low level of income at world level.

52.1% of the population lives in the coast, 36 .9% in the Andes and 11% in the jungle. Life expectancy in Peru is 69 years of age and at least 1,300,000 persons older than 15 years, are illiterate. Lima, the capital of Peru, houses around seven and a half million inhabitants.

POLITICAL ORGANISATION

Peru is a presidential republic with a State composed of three powers: the Executive, directed by the President of the Republic, elected for a five year period; the Legislative, formed by only one house of representatives (120) elected for five years; and the Judiciary, constituted by the Supreme Court, the Higher Courts and the First Instance Courts.

HISTORY

The land in which Peru is now located was inhabited 20,000 years ago by diverse groups of hunters and collectors, according to diverse stone evidences

Ancient expression of stone art of the Peruvian coast. Sechin complex, Casma (coast of the department of Ancash).

found in Piquimachay, Chivateros, Lauricocha, etc. Later on, other primitive societies developed during the years 6000 to 3000 BC until some of them became

experts in agriculture and in the domestication of animals, and established themselves in a sedentary way around the year 3000 BC (Caral, Kotosh, Huaca Prieta).

The big, ancient civilisations that originated in Peru started a thousand years before Christ and later influenced the development of other great cultures. The Chavin culture that developed in the Andes, in what is now the department of Ancash, is considered the matrix of Peruvian cultures. Other cultures followed it: the cultures of Paracas, Moche, Nasca, Tiahuanaco, Wari and Chimu - among the most important ones - and finally the great Inca State.

The Incas established their capital in Cusco, and from there they conquered vast kingdoms and nations expanding over a large portion of South America. The name of the state was Tahuantinsuyu and the level of social and political organisation it reached, as well as its knowledge of architecture, astronomy, agriculture, etc., were vast and notable.

The Spanish conquest of Tahuantinsuyu, brought down one of the most important cultures of the ancient world and put an end to the autochthonous development of the population of this side of the continent, which up to that time, had not had any influence whatsoever from the Occidental culture neither from Asia. The conquest was carried out by a handful of soldiers whose technology and strategy in battle was by far superior to that of the Incas. Besides, the Spaniards came at a very favourable time for them, as a civil war was going on and all parts involved were enemies among them: the Inca brothers (Huascar and Atahualpa) were fighting for the throne, the local kingdoms wanted to throw off the Inca yoke, the dynasties that controlled the power in Cusco hated each other, etc.

Feminine population, in rural zones, constitutes the largest segment of illiterate population.

Andean Peruvians exorcise the trauma of the conquest through mestizo dances in which they recreate Indian and Spanish characters, where the first mentioned make fun of the latter.

The trauma of the conquest that destroyed the Andean cosmos vision and generated a deep collective depression on the local people, also manifested itself in the grave demographic fall it caused. In 1532, the population of the Inca State was 12 million inhabitants. Less than one hundred years later, in 1626, the native population was 600 thousand. Although it is true that many deaths were due to the small pox and grippe epidemics brought in from Europe and to the exploitation of the Indians in the mines.

The period of the conquest lasted a few decades, during which the flashes of insurgency that appeared were put out in a sanguinary way, until the most important episode in Vilcabamba that put an end to the last Inca, Tupac Amaru in 1572. A civil war also broke up between the partners in the conquest, Pizarro and Almagro, which was gradually placated.

In was only in 1542 that the Viceroyalty of New Castilla was created, which later on became the Viceroyalty of Peru. After the fall of the last Inca in 1572, viceroy Toledo organised the viceroyalty in an efficient and prosperous manner, and thus it can be said that it was then when the colony period started. This was a period of great wealth and comfort in the viceroyalty, because Lima held the monopoly of trade with Spain and mine exploitation was at its best. Nevertheless, in the XVIII century the territory of the viceroyalty was divided, and the viceroyalties of New Granada with Caracas as its capital and Rio de la Plata, with Buenos Aires as its capital were created. With the two new viceroyalties, the trade monopoly between Lima and Spain came to an end and the Viceroyalty of Peru entered a period of deep crisis.

Towards the end of the XVIII century, a series of insurgent movements started, motivated by the ill treatment given to the Indians by the Spaniards. Rich mestizo Peruvians, whose economy was deteriorating because of the grave economic crisis, financed these movements. The most important of these occurred in Tinta, Cusco between 1780 and 1781, headed by Jose Gabriel Condorcanqui (Tupac Amaru II).

Representation of land owners during the celebration of the San Jerónimo fiesta, Cusco.

The Creole Peruvian oligarchy (Spanish descendants) was very comfortable with the peninsular power and never supported the insurgent movements, as did happen in the present Argentina, Venezuela, Colombia and Chile, were rich Creoles financed the war of independence. That is the reason why Peru was the last place to be liberated from the Spanish dominion and besides, by foreign liberators: José de San Martin was from Argentina and Simón Bolívar was from Venezuela. It was the first mentioned, José de San Martin, who created the first Peruvian flag in 1819 (after having landed in the bay of Paracas) and who, afterwards, on 28 July, 1821 proclaimed the independence of Peru, which was not definitely sealed until 1824, after the battles of Junin and Ayacucho.

The independence brought about a fight for power inside the Peruvian society, mainly due to the private interests of the leaders of the independence movement and the Creole power groups they represented. In 1825, Alto Peru separated, originating the Republic of Bolivia and in 1879, the

Balcony from where Jose de San Martin, Peru's Liberator, gave an earlier Independence Speech, in 1820. Huara, north of Lima.

unfortunate Pacific War between Peru and Chile broke out, same that meant the loss of huge territories and of some cities. The war was for the possession of the potassium nitrate deposits that existed in Tarapaca. Shortly before the war, Peru had experimented a slight economic boom as a result of the exploitation of guano from the islands, but with the war in went back into a new economic crisis.

During the XX century, Peru had democratic governments and military coups in power in constant alternation, same as in most of South American countries. The first migratory rush from the Andes to the coast started at the beginning of the XX century, mainly to Lima. The incoming foreign capitals and the modernisation of the country that required abundant and cheap labour provoked this. Later, at the beginning of the second half of the century, new migratory rushes started, motivated by the economic crisis in the countryside. The agrarian reform that began in the decade of the 60's, put the rights of possession of the land that was owned by few hacienda owners and owners of huge estates into the massive hands of the peasants. This generated a fall in agrarian production and the withdrawal of foreign capital, also driven away as a result of the nationalisation of the oil companies and other big industries at the beginning of the 70's.

1980 meant the return to democracy, but also the appearance of the terrorist phenomenon brought about by the Shining Path and the Revolutionary Tupac Amaru Movement groups; they were defeated in the nineties, but left the country even poorer that it was already and caused around thirty thousand deaths. The constitutional stability was disrupted once more in 1992, but was recovered entirely with the elections of the year 2001.

***Comuneros* (peasants)** parade during the celebration of the Peruvian independence anniversary. Puquio, Ayacucho.

PERU

The Peruvian Caballo de Paso (trotting horse). The horse, especially the Berberisco, the Arab and the Andaluz, came with the Spanish conquistadors and was the only means of transport for several centuries. Nevertheless, starting in the XVII century, several plantation owners from the coast began to select and crossbreed horses with the purpose of finding the one that would better react to the arid and hot geography of the northern Peruvian coast. They succeeded in developing this breed, which afterwards was taught a special way of trotting, that gives particular gracefulness and distinction to the animal, and great comfort to the person that rides it.

Procession of the Lord of the Miracles that originated in the XVII century during the colony. Next to the Pachacamac complex, in a place called Pachacamilla there was a settlement of Negroes and Indians. One of the Negroes slaves painted the Image of Christ hanging from the Cross (the same one that is now worshiped) on one of the walls of a dwelling. A strong earthquake shook Lima in 1655 and all the houses fell down in Pachacamilla, with the exception of the wall with the painting. Afterwards, in 1687, another earthquake destroyed all the buildings in Pachacamilla with the exception of the same wall. The inhabitants of the place attributed this to a miracle and the image has been worshipped ever since.

The brotherhood of the Lord of the Miracles puts together 20 groups of 120 devotees each and 2 groups of women singers and incense bearers.

The Acho Bullfight Ring. It is the oldest in America and the third oldest in the world. Don Agustín de Landaburu inaugurated it on 30 January, 1766, during the time of viceroy Amat. Before that date, the Spaniards and their descendants, the Creoles, who had been in this land for two centuries already, followed the bullfighting tradition and for lack of an appropriate ring, used the public squares and in some occasions they even conditioned Lima Main Square for the purpose.

The cockfights were introduced by the Spaniards. There are two types of fights: a beak fight and a razor fight. In the first one, the cocks wear an artefact tied to each leg (used to kill the rival with) but they use the beak to hold the adversary down. In the second one, they have a razor tied to the left leg to be used as a lethal weapon. The smarter one, not necessarily the stronger one, will win the fight.

Bullfighting has become one of the most deep-rooted traditions in all Peruvian towns, with Lima having the principal bullfight ring in America. The bullfighting fair of the Lord of the Miracles takes place in October of each year, in honour of the Patron of Lima.

Preparation of *anticuchos* in a popular typical fair.

Clay jugs to ferment the grape juice before distilling to produce pisco.

GASTRONOMY

Peruvian cuisine is very rich and varied. It is based on the abundance of agricultural products, fruits, meats and seafood that nature offers. Peru is a multinational country and its cuisine ascertains it. Each zone or region of Peru has its own dishes based on local products and the cultural legacy of the region.

The fusion with the Spanish culture after the conquest and the contribution later on of the African and Asian cultures during the colony and the first years of the republic, have played a part to enhance Peruvian cuisine even more, adding new dishes and flavours that have intermingle with the local customs creating new styles. A clear example of this can be found in Chinese food in Peru, which has been influenced by Peruvian taste and ingredients, modifying it from its original characteristics and giving it its own flavour: that of the *chifa*.

However, the dish that most identifies Peruvian cuisine at international level is the *cebiche*, which elaboration is not complicated, but precise what regards taste. Its origins go back to the fishermen than inhabited the Peruvian coasts, mainly in the North, who added salt, lemon juice, onion slices and *aji* (a kind of hot pepper) to fish meat. After a few minutes, the lemon juice penetrates the soft fish meat cooking it slightly and giving it an exquisite flavour, improving the natural flavour of fish and seafood.

Anticuchos are chunks of beef heart stuck on thin pieces of cane and grilled. They originate in the colony when the black slaves brought in from Africa used what was left of the slaughtered cattle to feed on.

In the Andes, the *cuy* (guinea pig) is the most appreciated animal because of its fine meat and

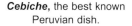

Cebiche, the best known Peruvian dish.

Traditional *chiri uchu* or cold spicy, typical Cusco cuy served in the streets during the Corpus Christi celebrations.

exquisite flavour. This animal was the protein base of Inca nutrition. It is easy to domesticate and eats healthy (only alfalfa and other vegetal species from the Andes). At present, the two most popular ways or cooking them are: one, stuffed with a herb called *huacatay* that gives it an exceptional flavour, and roasted, and the other one is fried or *chactao* where the animal is covered with ground corn and fried in oil with a stone on top. In this way, meat and bones get cooked all the way through.

In the jungle, apart from the innumerable exotic fruits, the most appreciated meat is that of quite a large fish called the *paiche*. Its meat is very tasty as it lives in the waters of the Amazon River and its tributaries and eats basically fruit. Normally the people from the jungle season it with native species and cook in over a fire, wrapped in banana or *bijao* leaves.

PERUVIAN PISCO

In the year 1551 some grapevines were brought in from the Canary Islands and the South of Spain for the purpose of making wine in the new colonies. Nevertheless, the kind of grapevines brought in was not adequate for making good wine. Besides, the King of Spain, Charles III, concerned about a wine industry in the colonies that could prevail over the one in Spain, imposed very high taxes on wine produced in the colonies.

Thus, the Spaniards decided to elaborate *aguardiente*, a kind of brandy, with the grape juice. Most of the vines that came to Peru had been planted in the fertile Ica valleys, very close to the present city of Pisco, where the Piskos ethnic group lived and who, among other things, used to make clay jugs in which they fermented their alcoholic drinks. The Spaniards decided to use the same jugs to store the grape brandy they had begun to distil, reason why said *aguardiente* acquired the name of pisco.

LIMA

The capital of Peru is located in the junction of the occidental chain of the central Andes and the Pacific Ocean, over a series of plains irrigated by the Rimac and Chillon rivers and the valleys they form, in the middle of a vast peripheral desert.

It has a population of almost eight million inhabitants, nearly thirty per cent of the population of the country that has exceeded the capacity of the city's basic services, from housing and potable water to transport and safety. The biggest part of the national resources, the State's powers, labour and education opportunities, and services in general are concentrated in Lima.

Lima is a fascinating city of great contrasts. On the one hand, it has beautiful districts and residential neighbourhoods; its colonial style historic centre is one of the best preserved in America; it has numerous pre-Columbian monuments and extraordinary museums specialised in the different pre-Hispanic cultures, the colony and the republic; it offers a rich and varied gastronomy, specially what concerns seafood; it has a great variety of hotels of all levels and styles. On the other hand, the poverty of most of the population is made evident when crossing the city and reaching its outskirts, populated in great part by Andean immigrants or their descendants, who toil day after day to make a living in the midst of the most adverse conditions.

Excavations in the archaeological complex of Caral - the oldest city in the American continent.

PRE-HISPANIC LIMA

There are many archaeological sites within the Lima area corresponding to different stages. Caral, located around 150 km north of Lima, is the oldest city in the continent, about 5,000 years old.

The administrative and religious complex of Pachacamac, located 30 km south of Lima, belongs to a stage quite earlier to that of the Incas. It was built during different periods and a wooden idol by the name Pachacamac used to be worshipped there. It was a kind of oracle that

was consulted about the future. Even the Incas, after taking possession of the kingdoms of the central coast, kept the cult of this idol, only putting the Sun deity first as the most important deity. Pachacamac can be divided into three parts: the first or the oldest temple of a more rustic construction; the Temple of the Sun, which is the better preserved part; and the Temple of the Moon, or Aclla Wasi, of evident Inca manufacture.

The people of Lima have got used to looking at - as part of the urban scene - a series of huacas or pre-Hispanic

View of Aclla Wasi, the central patio and the royal dwellings in Pachacamac.

Huallamarca (The Hualla ethnic group).

religious places scattered all over the city, as is the case of the Huallamarca huaca. This pyramid is located in the middle of the San Isidro district, and belongs to a period before the Incas. The Hualla ethnic group erected it for religious purposes. Some maintain that the adobes that cover its walls look like grains of corn, a sacred plant that was probably worshipped in this ceremonial centre. A small museum functions there.

CHANCAY CULTURE

This culture developed in the valleys of Chancay, 70 km north of Lima, between the years 1300 and 1400 AD. It is famous for its ceramics with the use of black over white and for its fabulous textiles, maybe the finest in this part of the continent.

Representations of fish, birds, monkeys and cats stand out in Chancay's ceramics, being its best-known pieces the jugs with vertical handles and geometric designs, as well as figures of birds, fruits and dogs. Also admired are the jugs with human head necks, modelled and painted, and even made-up which are called "chinas".

The most famous elements of its ceramics are those called "cuchimilcos", human representations slightly deformed in their proportions, generally with open arms and long legs ("patones" - long-legged), some with an open mouth ("cantores" - singers), and the unmistakably feminine ones. It is believed that their function was to preserve the soul of the death (they have been found in tombs).

Chancay textiles are of great quality and diverse techniques, as gauze, lace, tapestry, embroidery, brocade, prints and feathers. The motifs are recurring: marine figures, serpents, anthropomorphic beings. Brownish and dark colours predominate.

Chancay *silbador* (whistler), named for the whistling sound it makes when blowing through its spout.

Chancay anthropomorphic sculpture. The open-arms position suggests praying.

Ceramic representation of a priestess. Chancay culture.

Chancay character of political and religious importance on a litter or a raft.

Plaza Mayor
of Lima.

Lima was founded by the conquistador Francisco Pizarro on January 18, 1535, in the valley of the Rimac River ("hablador" - talking), very near the coast and at the foot of the Andes. Its location was crucial to conduct the conquest of the territories of South America and afterwards, to administer the Spanish colonies.

The urban distribution of the new city was made following the arrangement of a checkerboard, used already in England and Wales in the X century and made known by the Spaniards in the New World during the XVI century, following Emperor Charles V ordinances, that is, designing the city as a checkerboard where the perfectly square lots or blocks were distributed around a central square, called the Plaza Mayor.

Initially, Lima had an area of 117 blocks. The main colonial buildings, symbols of the new power, were located around the Plaza Mayor: the Church, the Government Palace and the Town Council. The square, located next to the Rimac River, functioned as a public space for civic and religious festivities, main city market and military concentration point at times of war.

Francisco Pizarro gave the best lots to the conquistadors and kept a block for himself, the one occupied by the present Government Palace. The Spaniards that arrived after the conquest were given only multifamily dwellings, known as *callejones*.

Pizarro Monument. This monument to the conqueror of Peru was erected on 18 January, 1935 to celebrate the fourth centenary of the foundation of Lima, and was initially placed in the atrium of the Cathedral. The North American Runssay MacDonald made this bronze and granite monument. Pizarro was born in Trujillo, Extremadura, Spain in 1476 and died in Lima, in his own palace (in front of the monument) of a cut in the throat given by Martin Bilbao on 26 June, 1541.

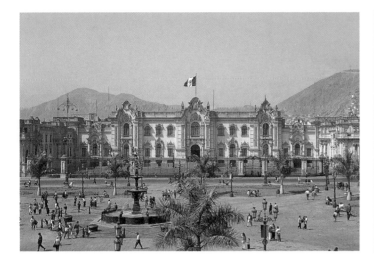

Left: Government Palace at the east side of the square. **Right: Stone Bridge** that joins two banks of the Rimac River (back of the palace). It was built between 1608 and 1610 in the same place where the inhabitants of the valley set up a wicker one, centuries before. Pizarro had a wooden one made that could not withstand very long the river's great volume of water, especially during the rainy season. It is one of the oldest monuments in Lima.

GOVERNMENT PALACE

Until 1587, the Palace of the Viceroys was a building of little architectural value and for that reason, the viceroy Count of Villar, commissioned Francisco de Becerra to remodel it. This new palace was completed around 1600, during the government of viceroy Velasco, and lasted without further problems until the earthquake of 1687.

Affected by continuous earthquakes, and rebuilt with variations in accordance with the styles in vogue, the Casa de Pizarro (Pizarro's House), as it is also known, was finally remodelled by the Polish architect Ricardo Malachowski and re-inaugurated in 1938 by the president General Oscar R. Benavides.

The palace consists of luxurious, marble rooms decorated with numerous pieces of art. The Colonial or Pizarro's Hall, the Great Dining Room, the Reception Hall, the Ambassadors Hall and the Minister Council Hall are among the most famous ones. It also has a chapel, a Sevillian patio, the president rooms and the presidential guard quarters.

Municipal Palace. The first Municipal Council was appointed on 22 January, 1535 and the first mayors were Nicolas de Ribera the Old and Juan Tello.

MUNICIPAL PALACE OR TOWN COUNCIL

When Lima was founded, the Town Council used to be next to the Cathedral, but during that same century it was relocated where it now stands.

The present Municipal Palace was inaugurated on 28 July, 1944 and Malachowski was also responsible for its design. Even though on the outside the building keeps its colonial style, its luxurious interior exhibits a predominantly French Renaissancist influence. Copies of the sculptures of Aurigas by Delfos and Saint Michael by Donatello are displayed in the main hall, apart from sculptures of San Martín de Porres and Santa Rosa de Lima - two Peruvians saints.

Main Hall of the Municipal Palace.

In the foreground, the bronze fountain made by Antonio de Rivas and designed by Pedro de Nogueras. Its construction was ordered in 1650 by the Count of Salvatierra and viceroy of Peru. Basilica Cathedral of Lima in the background.

THE LIMA CATHEDRAL

The church was built the same year the city of Lima was founded, and put under the patronage of Our Lady of the Assumption. In 1541 it was recognised as Church Cathedral by the papal bull of His Holiness, Pope Paul III dated May 14 of that year, and changed to the patronage of St. John the Evangelist. In 1545 it was given the category of Metropolitan.

Initially, it occupied only the lot that was assigned to it at the time of the foundation of the city; it was of a rustic construction, had adobe walls and a straw roof. Months later it was expanded to build a cemetery. Afterwards, at the arrival of Fray Jerónimo de Loayza, first archbishop of Lima, the original cathedral was demolished to build a bigger one, using *mangle* wood. This construction was concluded in 1551.

Nevertheless, owing to more ambitious projects and to the destruction suffered during the earthquakes that shook Lima at the time of the colony, the Lima Cathedral was redesigned and rebuilt in several opportunities until finally in 1758, the last reconstruction was concluded. The Austrian Jesuit Juan Rher was responsible for this work. He lowered the vaults down to the height of the cornice, replaced the stone vaults with oak wood and the crossings were made of cedar covered with plaster to give them the same appearance they had before (masonry). This was an old building system used in Lima, adopted then by Peruvian architecture again.

Choir chairs of the Basilica Cathedral of Lima. This is one of the greatest works of Peruvian art, which authors were Pedro de Nogueras, Luis de Ortiz de Vargas and Martín Alonso de Mesa.

Archbishop's Palace. Beautifully carved balconies of Moorish style decorate the façade of this building constructed in 1924.

TORRE TAGLE PALACE

The Torre Tagle Palace that dates from the beginning of the XVIII century, is the most complete, luxurious and beautiful colonial mansion in Lima. It is a work of art of Lima colonial architecture because of its perfect harmony: Andulician, Moorish, Creole, and even Asiatic contributions harmonise with incomparable charm. The architecture maintains the traditions of the XVII century, especially in the façade, the shape of the windows, the style of the balconies and the emphatically baroque style of the portico.

THE ALIAGA HOUSE

This house was built on top of the huaca or indigenous oratory of Taulichusco curaca (local governor). It is one of the most eloquent

Exterior balcony of the Aliaga House.

expressions of Limean architecture in its evolution through different epochs since the city was founded. The construction is contemporary with the city and belongs to the descendants of conquistador Aliaga, making it the oldest family real estate property in Peru.

The façade of the Torre Tagle Palace has the most beautiful colonial balconies of Lima. The Foreign Secretary Office functions in this building.

LIMA

The Osambela House. This house belonged to the marquises of Oquendo and Osambela. Its portico and the five balconies in a row are an example of the influence of what was known in Lima as "empire style". It was rebuilt at the beginning of the XIX century and the liberator Don José de San Martin stayed there after having proclaimed the independence of Peru on 28 July, 1821.

San Martin Plaza. This stone and marble plaza was built to celebrate the first centenary of the independence of Peru. The monument in the middle represents liberator José de San Martin crossing the Andes. It was made by Mariano Benlliure.

Alameda de los Descalzos. During its session of 6 February, 1609, the Lima Municipal Council agreed to build a tree-lined walk inspired in Seville at the foot of the San Pedro Hill that would offer an atmosphere of calm and relax. In the picture, one of the twelve Cararra marble statues brought in from Italy.

Centre and lower photos: Lima still keeps some colonial balconies of the many that used to fill its streets.

Baroque style façade of the San Francisco Church.

Beautiful Sevillian tiles. Pieces of the original construction of the Franciscan convent.

bolstered on the inside of the church. This main entrance is Lima's first retable-façade of the traditional baroque style.

In spite of the recurrent earthquakes that destroyed valuable samples of colonial architecture, this convent still has its original chapels and the tiles and roof decorations of its cloisters. The façade of the church, the sacristy and the choir are also the original ones. The high altar is a work piece of the architect Presbitero Matías Maestro (second half of the XVIII century) and the convent still has the cell of San Francisco Solano and his holy remains are kept there.

SANTO DOMINGO CONVENT

Its construction was started in 1547 on the lot assigned to it by Pizarro. The temple was built with bricks and lime and was composed of three vaulted naves. It was completed in 1599, in part thanks to Fray Salvador de Ribera, son of Nicolás de Ribera the Old, the first mayor of Lima.

The convent took longer to be completed, until late in the XVII century. The earthquake of 1746 destroyed the cloister of the noviciate; a work of Domingo Valderrama that dated from 1586, and its later reconstruction is quite different from the original one.

The dome was repaired in 1812 and a new altar was erected, this time of neoclassic style, under the responsibility of Matías Maestro. Its most valuable element is the tower, rebuilt at the end the

SAN FRANCISCO CONVENT

At the request of Fray Francisco de Machuca, in 1536 Francisco Pizarro agreed to cede the lots where the San Francisco church and convent would be built, in the same place they are now. At the beginning, as all the convents of the recently founded City of the Kings, it was quite a modest construction made with mud and wood. The first church, same which construction started in 1557, lasted 99 years, as it was destroyed during the earthquake of 1656.

The job of rebuilding the church was completed in 1672, and the Portuguese architect Constantino de Vasconcellos was responsible for it. The façade of the new church is among the best baroque architecture of the XVII century in Peru. Its portico stands out for its stone filigree, set between thick walls, rustically

Santo Domingo church and convent.

Jesuit San Pedro Church.

XVIII century, under viceroy Amat's direct supervision.

In Santo Domingo deserve special notice the beautiful convent (still a refuge of peace in the centre of Lima), the main cloister, the chapel dedicated to San Martin de Porres, what is left of the cloister of Santo Tomas de Aquino College and its beautiful interior patio,

with tiles brought in from Seville and laid down in 1606.

SAN PEDRO CHURCH (SAN PABLO)

The Jesuits established themselves in the lots where the church stands now and some years later initiated the construction of the temple. A second temple was built at the same time in what is today de chapel, called the Penitentiary and completed in 1574. The church kept on looking more beautiful as time went by, mostly thanks to brother Bernardo Bitt, who had worked with Michel Angelo for some time.

The construction of the new temple started in 1625, thanks to the fact that Father Nicolas Duran Mastrelli, Procurer from Rome, brought with him the drawings of the Church of Jesus with the idea they would serve as a model. It was completed in 1638, before the baroque style had come to Lima.

Even though it was originally called San Pablo, the great Jesuit temple of Lima is known today as the San Pedro Church. It survived the big earthquake of 20 October, 1687, without much damage to it; nevertheless a later earthquake destroyed its high chapel. Its best works are the retable, which are today among the best in the city.

Baroque façade of the San Agustín Church.

SAN AGUSTÍN CHURCH

Its beautiful baroque façade (XVII century) is all that remains as a testimony of its original architecture. The most valuable elements in the temple are the sacristy and the anteroom to the sacristy, renowned for the value of its carvings, furniture, pictures and roof decorations of the sacristy, that form a conventual complex of great quality.

Columns around the interior patio of the Santo Domingo convent, covered with tiles.

LIMA

Miraflores is a coastal district that faces the Pacific Ocean. Its modern, tall buildings rise above the Costa Verde cliffs.

The spirit of modernisation of the city has made it expand further South, where Miraflores stands as one of its most beautiful residential and commercial districts. Its beauty comes, in great part from its many well-kept gardens and its closeness to the sea that offers a beautiful sight of the Pacific Ocean.

Sunset at Parque del Amor (Love Park) in Miraflores.

Photos on the left: The big contrasts of the city of Lima become evident at its beaches: while the majority of people enjoy summer in the popular Costa Verde (right), the privileged escape South to places like the beautiful Embajadores beach (left).

THE LIMA MUSEUMS

Lima has a large number of museums that cover the different periods of this country's history, from the start of human activity to the pre-Hispanic, colonial and republican stages. The most important ones are those that cover the cultural expressions of ancient Peruvians that established notable civilisations between the years 2000 BC and the arrival of the Spaniards.

We indicate below four of the principal museums in accordance with the importance of their displays, two pertaining to the state and two private ones.

NATIONAL MUSEUM OF ANTHROPOLOGY, ARCHAEOLOGY AND HISTORY

It was inaugurated on 17 December, 1924 as the "Museo Bolivariano" and is located in the Magdalena Palace, which construction was ordered by viceroy Joaquin de la Pezuela in 1818.

It has quite a didactic exhibition that begins with the population of America, the origins of the culture in the central Andes and the first inhabitants of the coast, going through its Formation period, where the Kotosh and Chavin ceramic works stand out. The most important objects in the exhibition are the Estela of Raymondi and the Tello Obelisk (both belong to the Chavin culture).

It includes the regional developments of Nasca, Recuay, Pasash, Moche, Tiahuanaco and Lima; covers the sophistication and complexity reached by the Wari culture; shows the metallurgic work of the different periods in the room called "Metalurgia y Maestros Orfebres" (Metallurgy and Metal Workers). Exhibits textiles from different Peruvian

Above: Sipan ear ornaments. Rafael Larco Herrera Museum.
Above right: Erotic Moche ceramic figure.

cultures in the room "Tejidos Prehispanicos" (Pre-Hispanic Textiles) with more than 31,000 pieces; displays the Chancay, Lambayeque and Chimu cultures in the room "Reinos y Señorios Tardios", (Late Kingdoms and Nations) and finally, the Incas, in two exhibition rooms.

It has besides a gallery concerning the Peruvian Viceroyalty, with a chronological collection of paintings of the viceroys of Peru. It also has samples of the XIX and XX centuries' art regarding the evolution of the Andean culture.

MUSEUM OF THE NATION

The museum, founded in the middle of the 80's, does not posses a great collection, however its exhibition is one of the most didactic and well clasified. Its permanent exhibition covers four levels in a chronological and sequential way backed up by scale models, pictures and diagrams. The cultural patrimony pieces recovered from abroad are often exhibited in the entrance hall.

Ceramic bottle depicting a feline, Cupisnique culture, National Museum of Anthropology.

GOLD OF PERU AND ARMS OF THE WORLD MUSEUM

It was formed starting from the extensive private collection of Miguel Mujíca Gallo and includes valuable pieces of pre-Hispanic art, especially of gold, silver and copper, as also textiles. The most precious piece in the collection is the solid gold Tumi or ceremonial knife belonging to the Lambayeque culture, apart from necklaces, funeral masks, ceremonial vases, nose covers and miniatures. The museum also offers a peculiar collection of weapons.

RAFAEL LARCO HERRERA ARCHAEOLOGY MUSEUM

This undoubtedly is one of the best private museums in Peru, especially what regards its collection of northern cultures, the Mochica culture and its erotic art deserving special mention.

Rafael Larco Hoyle founded it on 28 July, 1926 in the sugar cane plantation (*hacienda*) Chiclín, Trujillo, and was transferred in the 50's to the mansion it now occupies in Lima.

The museum has two storeys and seven exhibition rooms, one vault and deposits open to the public.

The room of erotic art is in the first level, and congregates the largest number of ceramic objects of this kind in the world.

The rooms of the mummies, ceramics, metals, stone (where the Chavin temple serpent head and wrinkled man are specially interesting), textiles (including an extremely beautiful 2000 years old Paracas cloak and a fragment of cloth with 398 threads per lineal inch) and cultures (covering Peruvian cultures from the year 7000 BC to the Spanish conquest) are located in the second level.

The vault holds different pieces of gold, silver, semiprecious stones, specially ear and nose ornaments, breastplates, ceremonial vases and masks. The deposits contain thousands of pieces placed on glass-covered shelves, separated and classified in accordance to cultures, themes and series, so that the visitors may study them.

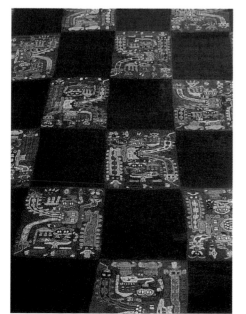

Detail of a Paracas textile.
Museum of the Nation.

PARACAS

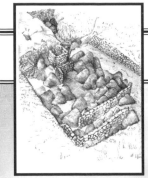

Paracas Culture

This pre-Inca culture developed between the years 1000 BC and 0, in the coastal valleys of the present provinces of Chincha and Pisco, on both banks of the Ica River. It had two stages: Paracas Cavernas and Paracas Necropolis, classification made basing on the way they buried their dead. The first and oldest one is strongly linked to the Chavin culture that existed almost parallel in Huari (near Huaraz). The second one, accountable for the beautiful textiles, is related to the Nasca culture that came after Paracas.

Up to 1925 when Julio C. Tello discovered the caverns and the necropolis in Cerro Colorado, the importance of this archaeological zone was unknown, since there are no signs of buildings or cities that could be related to cemeteries in this desert.

PARACAS CAVERNAS

What stands out the most about Paracas Cavernas are the painted textiles with designs of mythical beings of anthropomorphic and feline features, very similar to those found in Chavin. Entrance to the tombs belonging to this period is through a subterranean, 1 m in diameter cylindrical construction with steps at the sides, leading to a 4 m diameter pit that used to be shaped as a inverted goblet. Up to one dozen funeral bundles have been found in such a tomb; the mummies are in a crouched position, covered with beautiful cloaks of different finishing. Almost all of them show a deformed and trepanned skull.

CRANIAL TREPANATION

Cranial trepanation was very common in this culture; it was performed to cure wounds caused by bumps in the head, probably suffered during belligerent confrontations. A gold plate or piece of pumpkin shell was used to replace the damaged part.

Illustrations showing the Paracas tombs of the Necropolis (left) and Cavernas (right) periods.

CRANIAL DEFORMATION

As evidenced by the remains found in their cemeteries, the Paracas people used to deform their skull from birth using small boards and bandages to make it grow in the desired shape. Deformed skulls were probably part of a kind of religious ritual, or part of their customs, and maybe something that gave them prestige. Whatever the reason may have been, the Paracas mastered the technique to accomplish this, changing the axis of the brain and making it grow in an elongated, oblique way.

PARACAS NECROPOLIS

Paracas Necropolis came quite some time after Cavernas and was more developed too. The dead lie buried in chambers built over the ruins of earlier settlements. The burials are massive and the bodies were placed in a fetal position and wrapped with a series of beautiful cloaks, together with necklaces, ceramic pieces, gold, weaving and knitting instruments, weapons, corn, yucca and beans. The entire parcel is called a funeral bundle.

The best sample of the development of this period can be observed in their textiles of very fine and colourful decoration, with representations of humans, birds, fish and other animals, as also beautiful geometric figures. It could be established that during this period cranial trepanation was not very frequent. However, skull deformation reached its peak and the most used shapes were elongated and round skulls.

Paracas plate, over three thousand years old.

Paracas textile piece. Considered among the most beautiful samples of American pre-Columbian art. The magical, religious meaning of its motives goes beyond its formal beauty and among other things, it was a sign of distinction of the social and political hierarchy of the wearer of the cloak.

Above: The Cathedral. Rock formation shaped by the wind.

Above right: Flamingos (Phoenicopterus chilensis), birds that served to inspire the Peruvian flag: red wings, white breast.

Candelabrum: This enigmatic figure of 200 m impressed in bas-relief on the sand, is located north of the peninsula. Some speculations about its origins indicate that sailors or pirates made it to be used as a point of reference. What is true is that is has no connection with the Nasca Lines.

PARACAS NATIONAL RESERVE

Located in the Paracas Peninsula (230 km south of Lima), in the department of Ica, it is one the most attractive natural landscapes of the Peruvian coast. Its desert geography, washed by the cold waters of the Pacific, forms beautiful beaches of diverse sands and gives shape to the cliffs along with the wind. This place shelters a rich marine fauna and a great number and variety of birds (more than seventy) station there.

BALLESTAS ISLANDS

They are only one hour and 30 minutes away from the bay of Paracas and shelter various species of birds, seals and penguins. The high concentration of birds permits the accumulation of excrement, also known as guano, a very valuable fertiliser exploited by the State.

Humboldt penguins (Spheniscus humboldti). Species that has become acclimatised to the Peruvian coast.

South American fur seals (Arctocephalus australis) and southern sea lions (Otaria byronia) inhabit the islands.

TAMBO COLORADO

Front view of the complex from the ceremonial plaza. The name Tambo Colorado (Red Citadel) or Pucallacta derives from the reddish colour of its walls.

Beautiful and vast valley formed by the Pisco River. Tambo Colorado controlled the Inca road that connected Ayacucho with the coast, which is an indication of its military importance during the Inca expansion.

This pre-Columbian complex is located in the Pisco Valley, 30 km east of the detour of the South Pan-American Highway leading to Ayacucho. It was totally built of adobe during the XV century, when the Incas, led by Pachacutec, expanded their empire north of Cusco.

After dominating the local ethnic groups, specially the Chincha nation, the Incas found it necessary to establish a strategic centre to control their new domains, both in the administrative aspect as in the political-religious one. It

is believed this was the reason why they built such an enormous complex of geopolitical importance; there is also the supposition that Inca Pachacutec himself lived there to lead his troops during the expansion wars.

The complex has four areas or sections. The first one consists of the Inca palace, located north of the complex. The abundant ornamentation of its walls, the niches painted red and yellow and the human figures engraved over the alcoves, catch the eye.

The second section is located in front of the palace, and has an ample trapezoidal esplanade, probably a ceremonial plaza. The third one is next to the river and has three groups of buildings composed of dwellings for the lower class, food storehouses and military barracks.

Lastly, south from this building, there is a kind of military watchtower from where the whole valley can be observed. Its pyramidal shape with three rectangular platforms suggests it was a temple to worship the Sun.

Huacachina Lagoon. It is an oasis situated in the middle of gigantic dunes. The extension of the lagoon is 100 m x 60 m and palm and *guarango* trees ornament its shoreline. Popular tradition maintains that its waters are medicinal.

Beautiful interior patio of an ex-hacienda house. At present it functions as a hotel.

Extensive dunes form the Ica desert.

This warm coastal valley surrounded by vast sand dunes is located 300 km south of Lima, in the midst of one of the driest deserts of the Peruvian coast.

Ica was founded by the Spaniards in 1563, although not in the same location it now occupies. At first it was called Villa Valverde and subse-quently, starting from 1640, Ica. Since their arrival, the Spaniards exploited the rich and warm Ica valleys for agri-culture, using the local Indians that were conquered during the conquest. Before, the place used to be inhabited by small ethnic groups or *cura-cazgos* (small kingdoms), dominated by the Incas.

NASCA

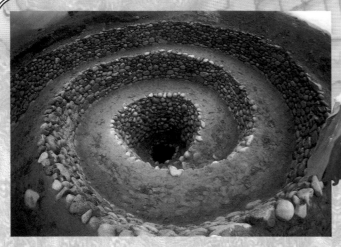

Feather piece belonging to Nasca under the influence of Wari.

Aqueducts. The Nasca were great farmers in the desert. They built subterraneous channels to transport water to their farms.

NASCA CULTURE

An important pre-Inca culture known as the Nasca culture, developed in the south of the department of Ica in the present city of Nasca, on the valleys formed by the rivers Grande, Ingenio and Nasca between the years 100 and 600 AD.

This culture became famous because of the renowned Nasca Lines, although it also has one of the most beautiful ceramics and textiles of ancient Peru. Its feather art, subterranean aqueducts and tenebrous trophy heads are noteworthy.

The Nasca people raised a series of buildings and pyramids (more than 30 in the zone of Cahuachi) of an elaborated building technique - they used earthquake resistant, conic adobes. It was a theocratic society influenced by neighbouring civilisations, like Paracas. They were later subjugated by the Wari culture coming from the southern Andes, event that modified the aesthetic patterns they used in the elaboration of ceramic objects and textiles.

Their decadence and later disappearance was probably due to the constant draughts provoked by the El Niño phenomenon that affected the Peruvian coast, and also by invasions and wars with other ethnic groups.

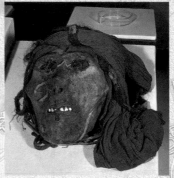

Trophy head.

TROPHY HEADS

The Nasca used to cut off the heads of their enemies, mummify them, sew their lips with thorns and wear them hanging from the waist. Supposedly, this transmitted to them the bravery and strength of the deceased.

TEXTILES

The Nasca culture textiles are very fine and elaborated. They developed various techniques and styles through their evolution (scholars distinguish up to five different styles). Initially their style was similar to the one of Paracas Necropolis, but they introduced three-dimensional needle knitting. Afterwards, they developed embroidery making the image "stand out". Subsequently, their iconography became stylised with the inclusion of mythical beings and geometrical designs. This is a fascinating style since the same cloth looked from one side shows a given set of figures, and upside down the figures look different. Later on it became abstract and geometric and finally, after the Wari conquest (700 AD), they developed new techniques as patches and batik.

FEATHER ART

These are pieces "knit" with colourful feathers, of abstract themes and mythological characters. These plume garments were sacred. The birds were related to the gods thus the clothes made of their feathers could only be worn by political and religious governors. These beautiful and delicate pieces of outstanding abstract designs and deepness of colour were made during the last periods of this culture and subsequently, under the influence of the Wari.

Nasca ceramic.

Nasca cemetery. The dead were usualy buried individually, although some collective tones have been found, where people of higher hierarchy were accompanied by their servants.

NASCA LINES

The higher concentration of lines, figures and trapezoids known as the Nasca Lines are found in the pampas of San Jose, 440 km south of Lima in the Ingenio Valley, although there are many others in the Palpa zone (north of Nasca).

Already in 1926 they were being investigated and archaeological informa-tion about these lines was being pub-lished, same that had been called "Inca roads" until then. Nevertheless, they gained fame in 1941 when the North American professor, Paul Kosok, announced to the world his "discovery" of "the biggest Astronomic Calendar in the world".

Hummingbird: Maybe the most emblematic figure of the Nasca pampas. It measures 96 m by 66 m. The Nasca attributed a divine character to hummingbirds, believing they were messengers between men and condors (which they considered gods).

NASCA LINES

Maria Reiche
maintained that the figure of monkey was made to mark the equinoxes.

Representation
of two llamas.

By measuring some organic objects found in the Nasca pampas using the Carbon 14 technique, it could be established that in spite of most lines corresponding to the period between the years 800 BC and 300 AD, some zones could have been worked before that time and others after it.

Maria Reiche, German mathematician and governess, who met Paul Kosok by chance in Lima, started a minute study and measurement of these lines at the request of Kosok himself. Thus, she became the most dedicated and concentrated scholar of the pampas and their mysterious contents, discovering many new figures and lines and contributing to their conservation as nobody else has.

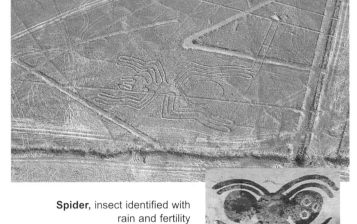

Spider, insect identified with rain and fertility

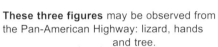

These three figures may be observed from the Pan-American Highway: lizard, hands and tree.

The *huarango*, coastal Peruvian tree was also part of their iconography in ceramics (picture on the left).

There are many theories that attempt to explain the meaning of the lines and almost all of them contribute to their study with some important aspects. Maybe the only refutable one is the one that maintains they were made by extraterrestrials and that the pampas used to be enormous spatial landing fields.

One of the explanations indicates that the lines were sacred roads that must have been walked on in peregrination, the trapezoids being ceremonial plazas. Paul Kosok and Maria Reiche sustained that these figures and lines could be related to the constellations, the solstices and the equinoxes and that their function was to serve as a great astronomic calendar.

Other investigators point out that the figures represent religious dance choreographies, other say that the images are representations of hallucinations of local shamans and also that they were part of some ritual to invoke the presence of water and fertility.

Among the figures that lay on the Nasca and Palpa plains there are fish, birds, plants, anthropomorphical beings and animals from the Amazon, the Andes and the coast.

Man with owl head, also known as the astronaut.

AREQUIPA

Arequipa Main Square.

Located 1000 km south of Lima on the southern Andes at a altitute of 2325 m, Arequipa is considered, along with Trujillo, the second most important city in Peru. It was founded by the Spaniards on August 15, 1540, represented by don Garci Manuel de Carbajal, Pizarro's lieutenant, in the valley of the Chili River and given the name of "Villa Hermosa de Arequipa" (Beautiful Village of Arequipa). A year later, it was granted the rank of City, as per royal mandate of October 7, 1541 of king Charles V.

However, the area had been inhabited more than six thousand year before by a pre-agricultural ethnic group, as confirmed by the petroglyphs of Toro Muerto. Afterwards, incipient and disperse civilisations of different stages of development established themselves in the area.

It was just at the time of the invasions of the Tiahuanaco-Wari culture of around the year 600 of our era, that a more advanced civilisation, that of the Collagua people, developed, same that originated the Churajón and Chuquibamba cultures (the latter having the influence of the coast from the Nasca culture).

AREQUIPA

Collagua cemetery in Chivay.

The devastating earthquake that struck Arequipa on June 23, 2001 seriously damaged the cathedral and other buildings in the zone. One of the towers felt down and the other got cracked.

The name Arequipa is composed of two different words: Are-quipa. If it comes from the Quechua, it means "Yes" (ARI) "Stay" (QUIPAY), while if it comes from the Aymara, it means "Peak" (ARI) "behind" (QUIPAY) or "Behind the Peak," in reference to the Misti Volcano, that crowns the city.

After it was founded, Arequipa was immediately populated by the Spaniards,

being the city with the highest concentration of Hispanic people of all Viceroyalty of Peru, as compared to Indian population. The city was built with white *sillar* (volcanic stone) which is plentiful in this volcanic region, reason why it is also known as the "White City".

Arequipa, as well as Moquegua and Tacna, is located in the Southern Volcanic Mountain Range and the city is built on

the slopes of the Misti Volcano (5825 m). This results in the ground not being very stable, and thus the city is periodically affected by earthquakes that have devastated it along its history, as the earthquakes of 1581, 1584, 1687, 1788, 1868, 1958, 1960 and the most recent one of June, 2001, among many others.

Inca terraces in Carmen Alto, Arequipa.

Above: The Misti Volcano seen from the district of Yanahuara. **Below:** In the foreground the Chili River gorge. In the background the Misti Volcano, that together with the Chachani and the Pichu Pichu Volcanoes, erects over Arequipa.

The splendid religious architecture and the lordly mansions of curved and tall fronts characterise the colonial architecture of Arequipa. This can also be appreciated on the side doors of the Churches of the Compania and Santo Domingo.

The buildings with curved ornamentation based on interior vaults, the sunny patios without corridors, extended to one side of the centre of the door, the cloister-like atmosphere of the inside rooms with stone vaults, also stand out.

The absence of materials like wood and the abundance of volcanic stone have given the architecture of Arequipa its appearance, together with the use of vaulted ceilings and carved stone. The walls tend to be very thick for fear of earthquakes.

THE AREQUIPA CATHEDRAL

Its construction was started in 1621, in accordance with the design of the architect from Lima, Andrés de Espinoza, and was completed eight years later. It was destroyed by a fire in 1844 and rebuilt by don Lucas Poblete. All earthquakes affected it to a lower or higher degree, in spite of the stability provided by its seventy columns. It has three portals, two towers and takes up all of the north end of the Main Square. The style is Neo-Renaissancist and is totally built of white *sillar*. The high altar is made of Carrara marble and the choir chairs, the sacristy and beautiful pulpit are remarkable.

The Irriberry House (1793). Now it houses the cultural complex of the San Agustin University.

Baroque façade of the Moral House, one of the most beautiful samples of the colonial architecture in Arequipa.

COMPANIA DE JESUS

Even though the present church dates from 1650, it was originally built in 1574 by Gaspar Báez and destroyed in turn by the earthquake of 1584. It has two storeys and a single tower, one nave, two side aisles, one sanctuary and a choir loft. The façade is imposing because of its mestizo style with decorative elements of the local fauna and flora as well as a bicephalous Habsburg eagle. Images of Jesus, Mary and Joseph are represented over the friezes. At both sides of San Miguel figure there are carvings representing shells, Indian masks, and an Indian head adorned with feathers.

Above: The church of the Compania de Jesus. The temple devoted to Santiago Matamoros (Moor killer), who during the conquest became Santiago Mataindios (Indian killer), houses the ornamentation work of incomparable beauty. **Left:** Detail of the façade decoration of the Church of the Compania.

Side entrance to the church of Santo Domingo.

Cloister of the Compania de Jesus. Although now it is used as a commercial centre, it still maintains the original structure of its construction that dates from 1660. Its corridors are decorated with beautiful portals made of carved *sillar*.

Simple but beautiful church of San Francisco.

Temple and the convent of La Recoleta (Franciscans).

AREQUIPA

Cayma. Located close to the centre (4 km), this district is known as the balcony of the city due to the splendid views of Arequlpa II offers. The picture shows the belfry and the central cross of the temple of San Miguel Arcangel (1730).

Church of San Juan (1750) in Yanahuara. District of small and narrow streets, located just 2 km from the centre of the city.

Spanish mill of Sabandía, constructed in 1621 by Francisco Flores, a well known stonemason.

Series of *sillar* arches in the Yanahuara viewing platform. In the background the Misti Volcano.

CONVENT OF SANTA CATALINA

Confessionals of the convent. Beautiful frescoes with Bible scenes decorate the walls of the cloisters.

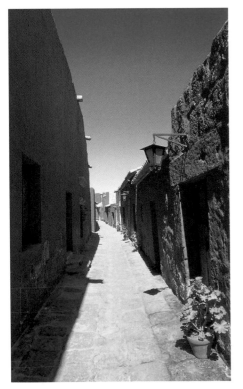

Zocodober Plaza, which name comes from the Arabian word "zoco" meaning interchange. Every Sunday the nuns used to gather here from very early in the morning to interchange the threads, cloths and other objects they were producing.

The monastery consists of three cloisters and approximately one hundred cells distributed along six streets and one passage.

In 1579, Dona María de Guzmán, a wealthy widow with no children, became the great benefactor of the convent, donating all her possessions and wealth for the construction of the "Private Monastery for Nuns of the Order of Saint Kathleen of Sienna". Once ready to be lived in, she herself entered the convent becoming its "first resident and prioress".

The group of buildings that make up this convent-citadel of more than 20,000 m², are built of the volcanic stone typical of Arequipa structures. The architectural style is that of the churches and colonial houses of the city, that is, colonial mestizo, with high and wide walls, and the common use of abutments to make the buildings more solid.

The citadel of this monastery began to extend because the earthquakes that

Opposite page: Cloister of Los Naranjos, constructed in 1638. Since then the nuns have kept the tradition of performing in three crosses the passion of Christ during the Holy Week.

Sevilla street. On the left the name of the person that used to live in this cell can be read. The kitchen that occupies the old church of Santa Catalina at the background.

continuously affected the city destroyed the communal bedrooms, and the relatives of the nuns that were secluded in the convent, the majority of which were well off, built individual cells. Besides, social differences were observed in the convent, situation that was reflected on the arrangement of the cells.

The Monastery has an impressive collection of paintings with works of great value pertaining to the Cusco School. Most of the works have religious themes, and this collection is considered one of the largest among Peruvian colonial art in the world.

Since the convent was founded and up to the year 1964, all the nuns that entered it were born in the colonies, none of them was Spanish. Only in that year were the first Spanish nuns admitted in the convent.

THE COLCA CANYON

By the side of the canyon this Collagua woman poses with her eagle.

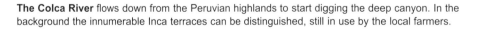

The Colca River flows down from the Peruvian highlands to start digging the deep canyon. In the background the innumerable Inca terraces can be distinguished, still in use by the local farmers.

The Colca Canyon. In the place called Cruz del Condor (the Condor Cross) the canyon reaches the depth of 1400 m.

The Colca River originates in the highlands south of Peru, at more than 5000 m.a.s.l. It runs through valleys and canyons, crosses the western Andes and reaches the Pacific Ocean after having travelled 450 km. The deepest part of its course goes down three thousand meters, making the famous Colca Canyon (100 km long), one of the deepest of the planet.

The Colca Valley is located in the Province of Caylloma, which capital is Chivay. Thermal baths of medicinal properties can be found there. The zone is rich in metals, specially silver, gold, tungsten and lead as well as minerals like gypsum, quartz and clay. These minerals were known and exploited by the Incas and later on, by the Spaniards.

THE COLCA CANYON

Condor flying above the Colca Canyon.

Majestic condor, 3 m wide, flying from its nest in the middle of the canyon.

Andean condor (Vultur gryphus).

Wide opened wings and claws prepared for the carrion. Condors are not hunters, only eat dead animals.

PUNO

Panoramic view of the city of Puno and Lake Titicaca. The monument on the left (seen from the back) corresponds to Manco Capac, the founder of the Inca State, who, according to a legend, emerged from the waters of this lake sent by his father, the Sun.

Puno is the capital of the department of the same name, renowned in the world for being located next to the highest navigable lake in the world, Lake Titicaca.

The city and the lake are located at 3827 meters above the see level and the inhabitants of the zone have adapted quite well to the geographic and climatic conditions of the area. Their copper skin withstands the inclemency of the glacial night and the strong, burning sun of the day. Fortunately, the lake provides a microclimate around it, because the sun heats the water during the day and at night the stored heat mitigates the low temperatures, creating a small zone adequate for agriculture. Besides, the lake offers cheap and easy to get food: fish.

The geography of the department is quite different from any other in the

Two Aymara women are selling fish extracted from the lake.

Andes. A great part of its territory is located on an almost uniform plain varying between 3850 to 4000 m of altitude. The highland and the lake are shared with the neighbouring country, Bolivia, as well as the language (Aymara) and the

ethnic group of the zone, the Aymara.

This flat geologic structure is surrounded by several mountain chains: the Real (to the south, in Bolivia), the Carabaya (to the north), the Eastern (towards the Puno jungle) and the Occidental Maritime or volcanic mountain chain (bordering the departments of Arequipa, Moquegua and Tacna). Only *ichu* (grass that grows above 3000 m in the Andes) grows in the cold pampas of Puno, same that feeds the South American animals of the camel family that abound in this region.

Nevertheless, the rivers that drain away Lake Titicaca also create a series of microclimates favourable for growing agricultural products, mainly potatoes, *quinua*, barley, oats and beans. These microclimates are also adequate for cattle raising, as grass can be grown to feed basically bovine cattle (predominantly).

PUKARA CULTURE (250 BC - 380 AD)

This is the most multifaceted ancient culture established in the north basin of Lake Titicaca, which now bears the same name, Pukara. Finely finished textiles of geometric designs and excellent rock sculptures have been found in this archaeological site of an extension of six square kilometres, which ceremonial architectonic arrangement points towards an advanced stage of development and social organisation. This social organisation influenced the level and style of its buildings, from the most simple and functional ones found in scattered villages, to the finely elaborated ones found in the centre of the settlement.

Pukara means fortress, and its walls do give the impression of being defensive fortifications. However, the most remarkable works are the sculptures made of carved stone and the anthropomorphic monoliths that are not found elsewhere in the south of Peru. The presence of the set of steps symbol, totemic animals (condor, felines, alligators) and human figures like the "Devourer," can be appreciated, same that definitely relate this culture to that of Chavin (north of Peru) and Tiahuanaco, that came later. The scholars also suggest that its influence reached the north zone of Cusco, the southern Peruvian coast (Moquegua) and the north of Chile.

High relief Pukara sculpture.

Pukara vessel.

TIAHUANACO CULTURE (500 AD - 900 AD)

The nucleus of this important culture is located 20 km south-east of Lake Titicaca, in Bolivia, but its area of influence reached as far as Lambayeque (Lambayeque culture), Lima (Lima, Ancon, Chancay cultures), Ica (Ica, Paracas and Nasca cultures), Ayacucho (Wari), Cusco and all the highland plain.

The archaeological complex of Tiahuanaco is colossal; deserving special mention its famous Puerta del Sol (Sun Gate), Puerta de la Luna (Moon Gate), huge monoliths, protruding heads, etc. Most probably this was the residence and ritual centre of an important religious lineage, a theocratic society that also developed ceramics, textiles and metallurgy.

Sun Gate or Inti Punku.

The Tiahuanaco culture achieved excellence in architecture and in stone sculpture. The iconography of its engravings include anthropomorphic creatures, felines, serpents and condors, geometric designs, steps, and spirals. The stylistic, cultural Tiahuanaco complex conforms the medium Peruvian horizon (not as old as some scholars indicate) but with a significant influence in Peru through the expansion of the Wari culture. Something worth mentioning about this culture is that they buried their death in an horizontal position (lying down) while in other earlier and later Peruvian cultures, the dead were buried sitting down, in a fetal position.

Monolith of an anthropomorphic deity, with hands over the solar plexus.

Tiahuanaco kero or ceramic ceremonial beaker.

Monolith engraved on andesite representing a mythological creature.

Temple of Fertility. Chucuito. Some scholars indicate that the Collas made these phallic images, while others sustain that they correspond to the period of the Inca domination in the zone.

Exterior walls of the Temple of Fertility. Lake Titicaca in the background.

The *chulpas* or funeral chambers with a cornice on top. They vary between 10 to 13 m in height.

"Solar circles" in the complex of Sillustani, location where religious or maybe funeral rites took place.

The Incas (Quechuas) named Collaysuyu the region of the Titicaca, where the Collas originated. This ethnic group developed in small kingdoms or *curacazgos* that occupied the place a long time before the Incas appeared. The most important were the kingdoms of Hatuncolla, Lupaca (Chucuito), Paucarcolla, Pacaje and Azángaro.

In the reign of Pachacutec, the Incas invaded and conquered the zone of the Collao and defeated the most important kingdom, the Hatuncolla one, led by Colla Capac. His empire reached as far as Arequipa and the north coast of Chile. The Incas displayed great cruelty with this kingdom to persuade the other kingdoms to surrender to the Cusco power.

Chulpas **of Colla origin in Sillustani**, with the Umayo Lake at its side (28 km north of Puno).

LAKE TITICACA

Dawn over the lake in Puno.

The first sunrays light up the lake port. Two refurbished old vessels of the XIX century, now in service, are anchored next to the piers.

Floating Uros island.

The islands have been repopulated with people coming from Puno and nearby towns, to make a living from tourism.

Ducks are hunted and dried in the sun. This is one of the most important foods in the islands.

THE UROS

They used to be a nation that lived on floating islands on Lake Titicaca. Nevertheless, the last of its members disappeared from the place in the second half of the XX century. The Uros did not have many opportunities to progress in the con-

LAKE TITICACA

Totora **reeds** were also employed to make the rafts used by the Collas, the Incas and the Uros to navigate in the lake. This custom still goes on today.

These little girls were born in these islands and are the new inhabitants of the floating islands.

Andean flamingo
(Phoenicoparrus jamesi)
waking on the reeds of a
floating island searching
for food.

ditions they were living in, and tourism was not an important activity then. For this reason, they took on the occidental culture and migrated to Puno and other cities that offered them a better life.

The Uros used to speak Aymara as their mother tongue (they were Collas) but could speak Quechua perfectly well, language that was introduced during the time of the Incas. They used *totora* reed remarkably well, plant that grows naturally in the lake, to make floating islands that were tied to the reeds under the water. Every certain time, the reeds had to be renewed, because with the passing of time, the sun and daily use, it began to sink. They used to fish and hunt for birds of the lake and even eat the reeds, as they do it again.

Cantuta (Cantua buxifolia), sacred flower of the Incas.

TAQUILE AND AMANTANI

According to the oral Andean tradition, the founders of the Inca Empire emerged from Lake Titicaca, and this may be the reason why the Quechuas have inhabited these islands since then. Taquile is one of the Peruvian islands of the lake, located 35 km from Puno. Around 2000 people of Quechua origin, language and way of life live there, maintaining their rigid traditions and keeping apart from the influence of the occidental culture. The most remarkable characteristic about their customs is the social organisation of the island, which is based on communitarian collectivism.

During the colonial times, the island went

At the edge of the road, these three small shepherds rest, while their flock (not in the photo) grazes near by.

Two Taquile community men observe the departure of visitors in the port. At the beginning of the XX century, this island was used as a political prison by several governments.

Amantani women get together to discuss community matters.

Amantani Island, Taquile's neighbour. The way of life and sense of community are similar to those in Taquile.

into the hands of the Spanish Count Rodrigo de Taquila (from which its name derives), who forced the inhabitants to dress in the fashion of Spanish peasants, so as to sell them their clothes himself. For this reason and until today, the inhabitants of Taquile dress in a different way than the rest of the peasants of the Peruvian Andes.

Woman wearing the "negrita" mask.

The passion of the Puno people to participate in these celebrations, make them save money all year round to be able to buy the dresses they will wear during the Fiesta de la Candelaria. Many of the dresses are worth over one thousand dollars each.

museo oro del perú
peru's gold museum

Puno *diablada* - regional dance).

...cession of the Virgin through the streets of Puno and the dance contest, where the best groups of dancers are awarded. The groups are made out of more than one hundred persons (some groups reach 500 each) and all together make around five thousand dancers and musicians.

The Candelaria is the biggest and most impressive folkloric fiesta that takes place in Peru, reason why Puno is called the capital of Peruvian Folklore.

CUSCO

INCA CULTURE

The Quechuas started out as a local kingdom called Marcavalle, around the year 1000 BC. Later on, an evolution took place in the ethic groups that formed this culture, originating more developed stages, as that of Killki and Lucre toward the year 1100 of our era; this is when clearer signs of what would be known later as Inca, began to show up.

The Incas went through a first local stage that started with the founding of Cusco by Manco Capac, around the year 1250 AD and lasted until 1438, when the ninth Inca, Pachacutec, started the second period: the expansion. This period was truncated in 1533 with the dead of the last Inca, Atahualpa, killed by the Spanish conquistadors, led by Francisco Pizarro. Therefore, the splendour of the Inca culture lasted only 100 years, period during which they built a vast multi-national state, conquering thousands of kilometres and hundreds of local kingdoms. They also reached a great level of development what concerns art, architecture and social organisation.

SOCIAL ORGANISATION

The Incas established the *Ayllu* as the nucleus of society, formed by large families or groups of individuals linked by family bonds (common origin, descendants of a same ancestor) that possessed land. This type of social organisation already existed in some pre-Inca cultures, only that the Incas made it extensive to their whole territory and more

Inca ruins of Inga Pirca in Ecuador. Huayna Capac built this complex during his expansion to the north that reached what is now Colombia.

Inca *quipu*. This system of knots on cords utilises the binary numeral system, and the Incas employed it to record accounting and other mathematical operations.

sophisticated.

When an Inca died, his royal family or descendants passed to form part of an special *ayllu* called *Panaca*. The function of the *Panaca* was to look after his mummy and preserve the memory of the dead Inca, using oral tradition and the *quipu* for that purpose.

The *Panaca* had at its disposal a numerous group of people belonging to different social levels, including women, servants, and priests apart from the family, all in charge of sustaining the power of the dead Inca. The mummy

of the Inca kept hold of all the properties, wealth and benefits the Inca had during his life, including his vast political power, as a member of the Cusco aristocracy.

The Incas divided Cusco in two halves, which they called Hanan (high) Cusco and Hurin (low) Cusco. This division had political and religious connotations as the Incas descended from families that belonged to one or the other half, thus generating rivalry among both dynasties.

THE ECONOMY

The system employed in trading operations between the people and the regions was interchanging or bartering; but apart from this, the State imposed the system of reciprocity and redistribution as the axis of its economic and

Inca jug or *aryballo* used to serve *chicha* (alcoholic beverage made with germinated corn) in important ceremonies. To keep it straight on the floor they made a hole on the ground to insert the tip of the base.

Inca wide-mouthed vessel with designs in high relief.

THE INCAS		
1.	**Manco Capac.** Founded Cusco around the year 1250 AD. There is no exact record of how long he governed, nor is there any record of the time each Inca governed until the ninth one.	6. **Inca Roca**
		7. **Yawar Huaca**
		8. **Wiracocha**
		9. **Pachacutec Inca Yupanqui** 1438 - 1471
2.	**Sinchi Roca**	10. **Tupac Yupanqui** 1471 - 1493
3.	**Lloque Yupanqui**	11. **Huayna Capac** 1493 - 1523
4.	**Mayta Capac**	12. **Huascar** 1523 - 1532
5.	**Capac Yupanqui**	13. **Atahualpa** 1532 - 1533

The Inca architectural characteristic that stands out the most is the inclination of the walls towards the inside and the trapezoidal shape of windows, niches and doors.

geopolitical development. Thus, agricultural work was performed for the farmer as well as for the State, both helping each other. In the same way, they conquered new kingdoms by offering them to participate in the State's economy, but after having submitted to the Inca and his laws.

RELIGION

The main Inca god was the Sun, followed by the god Wiracocha (the creator of everything), the moon, thunder, the mountains (*Apu*), condors and other animals and mythological creatures. The temples of worship were composed of *huacas* (sacred places), extending all over the Tahuantinsuyu, being the Koricancha the main Inca temple.

The Incas respected the local and regional gods of the nations they conquered, nevertheless, the conquered had to worship the Sun before any of their own deities.

THE INCA

The Inca was considered a living god and nobody could look at him in the eye. The king communicated with others only through his interlocutors. He dressed with the finest garments of vicuna fibre and the feathers of exotic birds, specially

made for him. He was carried on a gold litter covered with beautiful cloaks and multicolour feathers. Around him marched a retinue of guards, servants, musicians and dancers.

EDUCATION

Education was restricted to the noble classes. Men studied in the so-called houses of wisdom or Yachay Wasi, taught by the wise men or *Amautas*. These schools only existed in Cusco, where the sons of the politic dignitaries of the annexed kingdoms had to go from all points of the Empire. Women attended after a previous selection to Aclla Wasi or house of the chosen women. There they were taught the art of fine weaving and the preparation of the sacred *chicha* and were at the service of the Inca and their main deity, the Sun.

Inca textile work.

TEXTILE ART

The Inca textile art utilises a symmetrical, geometric iconography, with predomination of the colours white, red, black and yellow. For some scholars, the designs of the Inca ponchos were strongly identified with the family *ayllu* concerned. The Incas also created beautiful feather cloaks, vicuna and alpaca tapestries and cotton garments.

CERAMICS

Inca ceramics developed a style that imposed itself on the conquered kingdoms. Its charac-

Inca ceremonial wooden *kero* or beaker.

Inca plate with abstract designs.

teristics were the use of the colours black, white, yellow, orange and red, geometric decorations and polished surfaces. The best known examples of this ceramics are the jugs of different shapes: the ones with long necks and conical base called *aryballos* (*puyñun* or *macka* in the Quechua language), those with pedestals and handles, pots with one lateral handle, etc. The Inca style imposed itself or was imitated by local kingdoms originating, for instance, the famous Chimu-Inca and Chancay-Inca styles.

ARQUITECTURE

Inca architecture was characterised by the use of stones of different finishing levels, but with the same sense of sobriety, symmetry and solidness, in smaller, functional constructions as well in more symbolic and megalithic ones.

To this day, the big Inca constructions on mountain tops, where enormous blocks of stone blocks were carried uphill and put together without using any mixture between them and making them fit perfectly, still astonish the world. According to oral tradition, the Collas, of the highland region (Lake Titicaca) were the stone masters.

THE INCAS DURING THE CONQUEST

After having paid a ransom for his freedom, Atahualpa was judged and executed between June and July of 1533. Pizarro named Tupac Huallpa (called Toparpa by the Spaniards) as Inca successor, who died poisoned a few months later. Afterwards came Manco Inca, who after escaping from Pizarro's dominion, headed an Inca revolution and was defeated. He escaped to Vilcabamba, where he was assassinated in 1544. Next came Sayri Tupac, who after nego-tiating with the Spaniards, was poisoned. The Incas that followed were Titu Cusi Yupanqui and Felipe Tupac Amaru. The latter was the last of the Vilcabamba Incas, executed in 1572 by order of viceroy Toledo.

Qollqanpata Palace, the oldest in Cusco, built by the Inca founder, Manco Capac.

Cusco (3226 m) is located in the valley formed by the Huatanay and Tullumayu rivers, between the central and eastern mountain chains that form the Vilcanota junction between the Puno highland plain and the tropical mountain chains that enter the Amazon jungle (Quillabamba in the north and Paucartambo towards Manu in the south).

It was the capital of the largest and most powerful State ever to occupy the South American continent, the Inca Empire; there still remains a large amount of archaeological evidence that tells about its glorious and majestic past, in spite of the depredation and damage suffered during the conquest wars and the colony.

The Spaniards changed the original Quechua name of "Qosqo" into Cusco, as they were unable to pronounce the Inca language. It means "navel of the world," which was the implication the Incas wanted to give it when extending their territories; to the north, these reached the Pasto junction in Colombia, and to the south, the rivers Maule and Bio Bio in Chile. The Incas named their Empire Tahuantinsuyu, meaning the four parts of the world: Chinchaysuyu (north), Antisuyu (Cusco

jungle), Collasuyu, (Lake Titicaca region) and Cuntisuyu (now Arequipa).

The Incas gave the city the shape of a puma, an Inca deity. The head was formed by the Sacsayhuaman hill, the trunk by the Tullumayu and Saphy rivulets, and the tail by the confluence of both rivulets, same that originate the Huatanay River.

Its central squares, Huacaypata or the square of weeping, and Cusipata or the square of joy, formed the centre of Cusco; a broken, ceremonial pyramid stood between them. Around them were the Inca palaces, the Aclla Wasi (house of the chosen women) and the Suntur Wasi

(round house, house of weapons).

The few walls and rooms of the Inca palaces and buildings remaining today, served as foundations to the Spanish constructions. Almost everything was destroyed during the conquest and the colony. Even before the Spaniards arrived, during the war for the power between the Inca brothers Atahualpa and Huascar, sons of Huayna Capac, a great part of the city was destroyed. Atahualpa's Quito troops (the *Quitus*) had taken Huascar prisoner, looting and burning Cusco and its palaces, and killing every member of the family of the defeated Inca.

The building on the left corresponds to the present Archbishop's Palace of Cusco, constructed above what used to be the palace of Inca Roca.

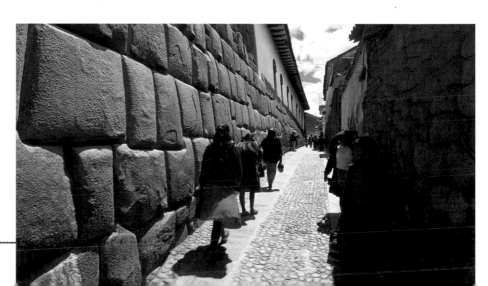

Koricancha or Inca Temple of the Sun. The Dominicans built their church and convent, Santo Domingo, on top of it.

The temples still existing are those dedicated to worship thunder and the rainbow.

The finishing of the stone works is magnificent.

KORICANCHA

This used to be the main Inca temple and its name means Gold Palace. It was built by Manco Capac towards the year 1250, with the god Wiracocha as the maximum deity. Afterwards, around 1440, Inca Pachacutec renovated and transformed it, the god Sun becoming the maximum Inca deity, dedicating the main room inside the temple to him. It also held rooms dedicated to revering the moon (*quilla*), the stars, thunder, etc.

The Spaniards that had the opportunity to see the temple before it was destroyed and looted, wrote that it was the most wonderful thing they had ever seen, even in Spain - walls covered with gold and precious stones, multicoloured feather cloaks covering the ceilings, etc.

Church of San Blas.

The Jesuit Church of the Compania de Jesus.

The Spanish conquistador Francisco Pizarro founded Cusco on 23 March, 1534, and proceeded right away to distribute the different plots among the conquistadors. The Church was the first to receive a plot to build the cathedral. This building was at first rudimentarily constructed over the old Inca Wiracocha temple. Nevertheless, the construction of the sumptuous temple that would be the Cathedral started in 1560, with Manuel de Veramendi in charge. It was completed in 1654. The church contains real jewels of the baroque-mestizo art, notable paintings belonging to the Cusco School, and the choir chairs, attributed to Diego Arias de la Cerda, is magnificent.

The Church of the Compania de Jesus was built in front of Cusco's main square, alongside the Cathedral, on what used to be the palace of Huayna Capac. It was started in 1581 and completed in 1671. It has only one nave and six

Cusco's Main Square during the Corpus Christi procession.

Cusco Cathedral
and Main Square.

Right:
Comuneros
(peasants) wearing
their best clothes,
carry the weight of
the platform in the
Corpus Christi
procession. They
walk barefoot as a
kind of self-punish-
ment to gain the
favour of their
patron saint.

Far right:
Corpus Christi
celebration. People
from all the parishes
arrive carrying their
saint or virgin.

lateral chapels. Its baroque-mestizo façade is beautifully made and is one of the most remarkable in Cusco.

One of the greatest works to be seen in colonial Cusco is the pulpit of San Blas, in the church of the same name (1562) in the Toqocachi or artisans neighbourhood. Its style is churrigueresque, and carved out of only one piece of wood, with abundance of details and a perfect finish. The work is attributed to the Indian Juan Tomas Tuirutupa, at it is said that the skull that crows the pulpit is his.

SACSAYHUAMAN

Three towers that reached four levels each crowned Sacsayhuaman.

The Inti Raymi, celebration that takes place every 24ᵗʰ June on the Esplanade of the Royal Lances in Sacsayhuaman.

SACSAYHUAMAN

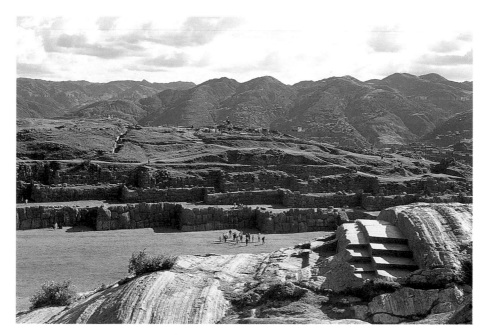

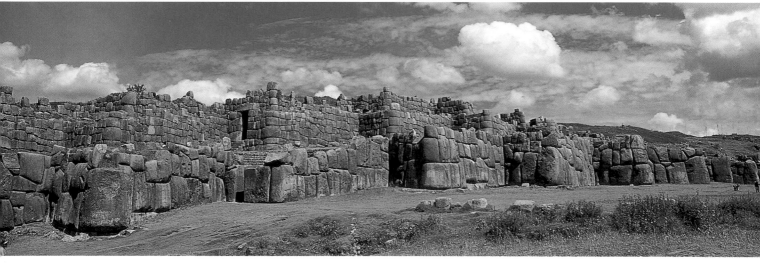

Built at the time of Inca Pachacutec, around 1460, Sacsayhuaman is one of the most imposing Inca monuments. It was called the Sacsayhuaman Fortress for a long time, but archaeological and historical documented evidence leads to think that it used to be a great political, military and religious ceremonial complex. It was probably erected to celebrate the military victories over the Chancas, hardened ethnic group coming from Ayacucho that invaded Cusco at different occasions.

Quechua experts and historians don't seem to agree on the meaning of Sacsayhuaman. Nevertheless, the mostly accepted idea is that it means "falcon, fill yourself up". Others indicate that it could mean "speckled falcon." This bird was an Inca deity.

The complex has three levels of ramparts in zigzag, with the biggest stones in the first level. It is surprising to see the perfection with which these stones have been put together without any mud mixture between them, as is also to imagine how these enormous stones were transported there and carried uphill.

There were three towers or edifications on top of the complex; one of them was circular and the other two rectangular. According to the chronicles of the conquest, those buildings were finely finished and covered with sheets of gold and silver and beautiful cloaks made of feathers from exotic birds, which gave the complex a beautiful and magical appearance.

Sacsayhuaman was destroyed during the wars between the conquistadors and Manco Inca's resistance and later on during the colony. For years it was a quarry from which stones were taken to build the Cusco Cathedral and other Hispanic churches and buildings.

The esplanade in front of the bulwarks used to function as a ceremonial square, called Esplanade of the Royal Lances and opposite it, there is a small hill (Suchuna) with seats carved on top, one after the other, which were supposedly royal seats from where the Inca conducted the religious and military ceremonies that took place there.

QENQO - TAMBOMACHAY

Sacrificial table in Qenqo.

Qenqo. Monolith representing a zoomorphic deity.

Above: Tambomachay. **Left:** Two Cusco peasant girls and their little alpaca in the surroundings of Tambomachay.

QENQO

Is located east of the Sacsayhuaman complex. It is formed by two monoliths carved in and outside, with some inscriptions in zigzag (from which its name probably derives) that stand out. It had a religious ceremonial function and was dedicated to sacrificing living creatures (probably llamas). This idea derives from the fact that there is a sac-rificial table carved in the lower part of the walls of the cave, with the zigzag mentioned carved on top of it, same that leads to the figure of a llama. It is assumed then, that the blood coming from the sacrificed animal fell on the zigzag and travelled to the figure of the llama.

There is also a semicircular amphi-theatre around a big stone block placed on a pedestal. The Spaniards damaged the shape of the monolith after the conquest, but its zoomorphic aspect (perhaps a monkey) is still evident.

TAMBOMACHAY

Leisure place built by Inca Tupac Yupanqui on the slope of a hill, with water coming from subterraneous channels flowing out of some efficiently arranged fountains. It has three levels joined by steps and corridors and a fine Inca finish, that is, the stones are perfectly joined together without the use of any mor-tar. Another characteristic is the inclination of the walls towards the inside.

THE SACRED VALLEY OF THE INCAS

The Urubamba River formed the Sacred Valley of the Incas when it connected the Pisac complex with that of Ollantaytambo, which were in turn, part of the natural road that, following that river, led to Machu Picchu.

The Incas assigned a sacred character to this valley, as their astronomers and priests sustained that it was a projection of the Milky Way, where the sacred Inca constellations - the llama, the condor, the tree, etc. - were situated.

In fact, a lot of energy concentrates there and its exuberant geography gives the scenario built by the Incas in the valley, a magic touch. The Pisac and Ollantaytambo complexes were not mere worshipping places, they were key places in the politic and religious organisation of the vast Inca State of the Tahuantinsuyu. The agricultural production of this valley had more of a ritual than functional character and its inhabitants were selected to be given the privilege of living there.

PISAC

Is located in the Yucay zone, at the right margin of the Urubamba River. Its name is associated with an apparently extinguished bird, similar to a partridge

The Sacred Valley of the Incas.

that used to inhabit the zone. The whole of the Pisac complex can be classified in three parts: the military one, formed by the fortress and the soldier quarters; the religious one, formed by the sanctuary and the Temple of the Sun and the city, where the dwellings of the chosen inhabitants of the place were located.

The military constructions and the fortress are strategically located over the second part of the mountain from which the whole valley could be observed. Its walls are thick and bent towards the inside, and the fact of being placed on a natural rock over 200 m long, gives the place an appearance of invincibility.

The sanctuary is located at the front of the first elevation of the mountain and has seven rooms made of finely polished stone. The Intihuatana or principal worshipping place consecrated to the Sun is in the middle, with a view covering the depth of the valley.

The city is made of twenty buildings of lesser architectural value, arranged in a semicircle at the edge of the mountain.

THE SACRED VALLEY OF THE INCAS

Ollantaytambo.

OLLANTAYTAMBO

Is located north of Cusco, at the other end of the Sacred Valley, very close to Machu Picchu. Two words form its name: Ollanta, the name of a soldier of the local ethnic group that served in the army of Inca Pachacutec and became well known when he fell in love with an Inca princess, and Tambo, meaning a place of rest.

The site was a complex of great importance for the Inca government, as besides forming part of the Sacred Valley, it was near the jungle zone of Tahuantinsuyu dominated by the Antis ethic group. The Incas were always fearful of the jungle and could not conquer much of it. The best food products for Cusco came from there, as did the exotic birds which feathers adorned the Inca's attire.

As a result of this, a big army had to concentrate at Ollantaytambo and in addition, the place had to serve as a royal palace where Inca authorities could negotiate and entertain the Amazon chiefs. This conclusion is consistent with what can be seen in the complex; there were numerous rooms to lodge the soldiers and the military, politic and religious dignitaries, rooms intended for the chosen women (Aclla Wasi) and big food storehouses, strategically protected.

Once more, it is surprising to see the enormous size of the rocks used in the construction of this complex, same that came from quarries located at the other side of the valley on the opposite side of the river, several kilometres away. How did they transport and carry them to the top of the hill? There is still no forceful answer to this question.

CHINCHERO - MARAS - MORAY

Chinchero. This town is located between ancient Inca constructions that controlled access to the Sacred Valley. There are a great number of terraces on the slopes of the nearby hills as well as portions of stone constructions scattered all over the place. The most interesting thing to be seen in the main square is the Inca wall with trapezoidal niches.

Maras salt pans exploited since ancient times, prior to the Incas.

Circular terraces of Moray. Located north-west of the town of Maras, composed of four circular, concentric terrace complexes. There is no record of when they were made, but it is presumed that the Incas made them (they are the only ones of their kind in Peru). This is a mayor engineering work, and the most surprising thing about it is that it was used to modify certain varieties of local agricultural products to make them more resistant to the climate. The different ecological levels created in the terraces, below ground level, were intended for controlling the environmental temperature, and it is presumed that each terrace was covered with soil coming from various locations in the Tahuantinsuyu.

Tipón. Beautiful terraces and water fountains are all that is left of the ancient palace of Inca Yawar Huaca. It is located south of Cusco.

Pikillacta (flee town). Is a big archaeological complex belonging to the Wari culture that populated this zone around the year 800 AD. Pikillacta was a great walled-in city with buildings, streets and squares. Thousands of people lived there in multi-family buildings; only the elite had individual, one-family houses.

Andahuaylillas. Small town located south of Cusco. Its small church (XVII century) is full of colonial frescoes.

Raqchi is located in the town of San Pedro de Cacha, very close to Sicuani, south of Cusco. It is one of the most beautiful and impressive Inca complexes, which function was to administer and store the tributes that were paid to the Inca in agricultural products coming from the Puno highlands (Collasuyu). This place also housed the most impressive temple consecrated to the god Wiracocha and palaces that served as residences to the noble class of Cusco and to the Inca himself, and a series of rooms to accommodate the troops.

Town of San Pedro de Cacha, next to the old Wiracochoa Temple, Raqchi.

PAUCARTAMBO

The Vilcanota River, that later becomes the Urubamba River. It comes from the highlands and flows to Machu Picchu.

The morning dew leaves its traces on the spikes of barley.

After the fiesta, the siesta, seem to mean this two inhabitants of Paucartambo, town located 100 km southeast of Cusco.

TRES CRUCES

A new day dawns over Tres Cruces, the last mountain on the Andes and the beginning of the Amazon jungle (covered with clouds) on the way to Manu.

Two *comuneros* from Q'eros. This community of peasants is one of the few still faithful to the Inca traditions and customs.

MACHU PICCHU

Machu Picchu in all its magnificence. The mountain behind the city is Huayna Picchu ("young peak"). The terraces for agricultural use, that also support the complex, can be seen on the left. The Principal Plaza is in the centre with the Intihuatana pyramid on its left.

It is located 130 km from the city of Cusco on the canyon formed by the Urubamba River, on the slopes of the hill of the Machu Picchu mountain, which means "old peak." This is not the original name of the city, same that is not known, reason why it bears the same name as the mountain.

This archaeological complex, one of the wonders of the world, remained hidden behind the mist of a humid forest of exuberant vegetation until the year 1911, when the North American explorer, Hiram Bingham, made public the famous finding of the ruins. Nevertheless, this place was known already during the colony and the first years of the republic, what is confirmed by several existing documents that make reference to it.

It was a sacred city where the chosen resided, probably the Inca nobility and the priests. The difficult access to the area made it secure, and the scenario around it gave it the enigmatic character it still has. However, during the conquest, the Spaniards never attacked the place, since the last Inca bastion was in Vilcabamba and not in Machu Picchu.

Orchids in Machu Picchu.

All evidences point to the fact that all its inhabitants abandoned Machu Picchu. They may have fled to the jungle because of the presence of the Spanish hosts. What is certain is that in the area next to the complex, there are a number of citadels as impressive as this one, which were also abandoned. All of them have the same characteristics: worshipping ceremonial stands, terraces over the hills, military sectors and royal palaces. Such is the case with Wiñay Wayna, Sayacmarca and Phuyupatamarca on the Inca trail, or Choquequirao to the north-west (and some others that were recently under the process of being explored and investigated, plus those still to be found).

Machu Picchu had two sectors dividing the city: the agricultural one and the urban one. The terraces around it, especially those south of the complex, formed the agricultural sector. The urban sector was separated from the agricultural one by a ditch and a wall, and there was a guarded entrance controlling access to it.

In the urban sector stand out the ceremonial buildings, the famous Temple of the Sun, as well as the royal palaces and the renowned Intihuatana, on top of the pyramid located north of the Sacred Plaza.

Bingham studied the complex closely and even made excavations, finding 173 human remains, the majority of which (one hundred and fifty) belonged to women. The North American explorer indicated that the ceramic, metal, textile and stone elements found were few, apart from having detected signs of looting at different points of the place.

Small Inca gold llama.

Terraces of the agricultural sector crowned by the Caretaker's Hut and higher up, the Machu Picchu peak.

This fact reinforces the hypothesis that the site was abandoned. However, Bingham found numerous pieces of ceramic scattered around under the Temple of the Three Windows, next to the Principal Plaza, which he sustained were probably dropped there as part of a worshipping or sacrificing ritual.

The urban sector concentrates a large number of buildings that were used as dwelling places. These are located at different levels facing east, in front of the Putucusi mountain. They are finely finished, two-level buildings, even though the stones used are not very big. The second storey had a wooden floor and the roof was made with wood beams held with rope on special indentations bored on the stone. The roof was thickly covered with dry straw made with the water-resistant *ichu* plant.

The wood used in all Inca constructions was brought in from the jungle, which made it very valuable. When the Incas abandoned a place (because of military strategy, danger or lack of interest), among other things, they always took the wood with them to be used again.

The urban sector presents a series of

The Temple of the Tree Windows. It is thought that the religious ceremonies and animal sacrifice took place here.

streets, passages and stairways that communicate the buildings with each other, in such a way that in some cases it is necessary to go through several chambers to reach a particular one. Evidently, the purpose for this design was to make safer certain areas of the complex.

MACHU PICCHU

The Temple of the Sun in the foreground. To the right, the Palace of Ñusta or Inca Princess. In front of the temple, the Putucusi mountain.

TEMPLE OF THE SUN

The Temple of the Sun is one of the buildings that displays the finest finish of all Machu Picchu. Because of the similarity of the curved wall with that of the Koricancha in Cusco, Bingham concluded that this temple had also been dedicated to the highest Inca god.

This temple has three windows, two of which permit the sun rays to enter in a precise way during the summer solstice (December 21) and the winter one (June 21), while the third one presents some perforations around its frame, reason why it is called the Window of the Serpents (which were probably introduced in the room through those holes).

The Temple of the Sun was built on natural rock, which was given shape on the lower part to carve a small mausoleum with trapezoidal niches. The exterior part of the rock was carved at intervals representing the three sacred spaces of the world of the Incas, the world of the death, the world of the living and the world of the gods.

Window of the Serpents.

Intihuatana in Machu Picchu. In the background Huayna Picchu emerges from the clouds.

INTIHUATANA

The Incas had cults related to agricultural periods that included sophisticated ceremonies, where their astronomical and engineering knowledge went hand in hand with their religious beliefs. The Intihuatana was the place designed for this purpose.

"Inti" means sun and "huatana" means a place to tie up. The translation of the terms would be "a hitching post of the Sun" And that was precisely what the ceremony consisted of. During the winter solstice, date which according to the calendar is the shortest day of the year, the Incas asked the god Sun not to forsake them, to be born again and start a new cycle of new and longer days. To do this, they had to establish their permanence in the cosmos using this carved rock to perform the necessary rituals.

The change of the solstice period is like the change from night to day. The day ends in night to dawn again starting a new day. Extrapolating this concept, each period ended on a date and a new one with better omens, should start. Therefore, the Intihuatana not only marked the change of a date, but it implied the cult of the supernatural to influence their new lives in a positive way. In the same way, they did not see death as the end of things but as the start of a new stage, which they expected would be better.

The Intihuatana was carved creating steps at its different sides and a central rod that comes out from its highest point. The steps represent the religious Inca spaces, same as in the Temple of the Sun (in the lower part). The rod that comes out of the block was carved taking into account certain astronomical measures that allow for the light of the sun to coincide with certain places during the solstice. The elevation of said rod can also be related to the peaks of the mountains, which the Incas considered sacred (Apu).

More than 250 species of orchids have been identified in the area.

MACHU PICCHU

Machu Picchu seen from Huayna Picchu. For some, the Inca city has the shape of a condor with spread out wings, the beak pointing south and the tail towards Huayna Picchu.

Temple of the Condor - Temple, prison or both ?

TEMPLE OF THE CONDOR

The Temple of the Condor is located in the eastern urban sector of the city and owes its name to the similarity existing between the shape of the construction and that of this bird. It seems it was the place, were the Machu Picchu jail or punishment cells used to function. Inside the building, there are some subterraneous cells and on top of what would be the wings of the bird, there are a series of windows that look like cells, with holes on the side walls to hold the prisoners by the hands through them.

For the Incas, the condor was a sacred bird, a god that was worshipped throughout the Inca State. As this bird eats carrion, it is possible that sacrifices were made to honour this god, offering the dead bodies of their enemies, whom they may have first tortured and then killed in this zone. These are just speculations made by some researchers in their efforts to explain the function of this building.

INCA TRAIL

Partial view of the Wiñay Wayna complex.

Wiñay Wayna on the Inca trail to Machu Picchu.

Small waterfalls in Wiñay Wayna.

The Incas build a vast road system that connected the four ends of the Empire with Cusco, the capital, and the inside towns with each other. The extension of all the Inca road is calculated in more than 30,000 km.

One of the most famous Inca trails is the one that goes from the Sacred Valley to Machu Picchu, north of Ollantaytambo that follows the Urubamba River, going through mountain chains, travelling more than 50 km. The highest crossing pass of the trail reaches the altitude of 4200 m.

Even though the trail had been used by the peasants of the area for a long time, it was Hiram Bingham who after his discovery of Machu Picchu during his search for Vilcabamba, informed of its existence in 1915. However, as from that year and up to the decade of the forties, the area was restricted for the purpose of supporting archaeologists and other researchers in their studies. In 1941, the Norwegian expedition, headed by Paul Fejos, made known the impressive ruins of the Wiñay Wayna ("forever young") complex.

Water fountains in the foreground going downward one after the other at Wiñay Wayna. On the mountain in the background the Inca trail can be seen on the edge of the precipice.

AYACUCHO

Inhospitable and desert geography of the Ayacucho heights.

Ayacucho (2761 m) is one of the cities and departments of Peru that have the highest level of poverty, low agricultural production and low life expectancy (under 50 years of age). Its geography is not generous in agricultural land, be it because of its steep Andean mountains or its freezing and desert heights. All this contributed to giving birth to the movement of violence that shook the country in the eighties and beginning of the nineties, turning it into a city surrounded by the violence of

terrorism coming from Shining Path terrorist group that unfortunately, made its appearance in this noble Andean land.

After these years of darkness, when the different populations of the area were being affected by violence, with thousands dead and enormous damage to public and private property, Ayacucho is now, once more, the beautiful city of marked colonial religious quality, with 38 churches that have made it famous as the "City of the Churches". However, it is

The saints and virgins of Ayacucho churches are taken out during the Holy Week and carried on platforms decorated with wax and silver incrustations.

Ayacucho Main Square, with the cathedral of renaissance baroque style (1615) in the background.

AYACUCHO

even more famous because of the deep religious feeling of its people, and the celebration of the Holy Week, which is very much appreciated in Peru.

Ayacucho is one of those few places chosen by "history" to act repeatedly. During the time of the expansion of the Inca State, the ethnic groups established in this area were the ones that exercised the most resistance to avoid that growth. The Incas had to fight hard to defeat the Chancas and the Pocras, and when they finally succeeded in doing it, they completely annihilated the population. That is why it is said that Ayacucho means "home of the death".

Another special event that took place on this land was the Battle of Ayacucho on 9 December,

1824, when the Spanish troops of viceroy La Serna fought against the Liberation Army of Peru. This battle meant the end of the Spanish presence in the old American colonies and sealed the independence of the new nations of this side of the continent.

Ayacucho was founded in 1537 by Pedro Anzures Henríques de Camporredondo, by decree of the conquistador Francisco Pizarro, and given the name of San Juan de la Frontera de Huamanga, for the purpose of serving as a place to rest during the journeys between Lima and Cusco (this city is also known as Huamanga, which in Quechua means "falcon, fed yourself up".

Multicolour grains of corn.

Monument in the Pampas de Quinua (3300 m) where the Ayacucho Battle that sealed the independence from Spain, took place.

Cactus plantation and imminent harvest of prickly pears (*tunas*).

Product exchange or barter, old Andean tradition still practised in Ayacucho and its surroundings.

Wari vessel with a double spout and connected handle.

WARI CULTURE

This important culture developed between the years 500 AD and 900 AD and succeeded in covering a vast territory that reached Lambayeque in the north and Moquegua in the south. Its capital and main religious centre was located in Wari or Huari (3000 m) 22 km north-east of Ayacucho. This was a huge city that included streets, squares, houses, storehouses and diverse platforms.

The urban development of the Wari is remarkable, and stylistic patterns of their development can be found in the sites they occupied. The cities they built were walled in and located in strategic places. They had internal squares surrounded by a series of buildings destined to multifamily housing, silos and communitarian areas. This leads to consider that a nation was concerned that planned and controlled its population, was well organised and had adequate administrative and economic knowledge.

The Wari nation conquered by military means a series of local states and could yet benefit from the influence of the Tiahuanaco highland culture that gave the people of Ayacucho its religious patterns and corresponding iconographic elements (present in textiles and ceramics). In their expansion, they transmitted the mentioned concepts and also introduced the binary accounting system of the *quipu* (later assimilated by the Incas), and constructed an important road system.

TEXTILES

Wari culture textiles are very fine and of a uniform and compact weaving. The use of bright colours (red, yellow) stands out, contrasting with ochre and black. The iconography is majestic, very imaginative and

Circular ceremonial amphitheatre, surrounded by diverse quarters. Wari.

Four-point cap used by important personalities or priests.

mostly religious, with the presence of the god of the staffs and a combination of abstract and geometric designs. To many scholars, the Wari iconography is more of an intellectual, ideographic instrument than a spontaneous decorating

expression.

They employed cotton and wool from animals of the camel family (including vicunas) and applied the techniques of brocade, warping patterns and painted fabrics, among others, including their remarkable tapestry, knit with very fine thread of up to 0.1 mm in thickness.

CERAMICS

Wari ceramics show also the strong influence of the Tiahuanaco culture. During the first period, they developed a style characterised by very large pieces; generally jugs for water keeping or large cylindrical containers for offerings, almost 100 cm high and 90 cm in diameter. Its common to find on the objects a band with representations of the Tiahuanaco iconographic elements, coloured in red, cream, purple, grey, black and white.

Wari priestess wearing a four-point cap.

New styles were developed during the Wari geographic expansion, like those seen in Nasca ceramic art, predominating the face-neck jugs, cups and images of animals and plants, keeping within the Tiahuanaco iconography. They also incremented the productions of functional ceramic objects with similar images but of a lower quality finish.

Wari ceramic works have been found in zones as distant from its main centre as Cajamarca and Lambayeque, where representations of felines of geometrical features, cups and face-neck jugs, stand out.

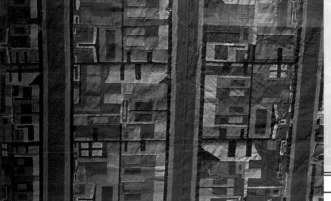

Wari textile work.

The Incas in Ayacucho

Usnu **or ceremonial broken** pyramid totally made of stone. It is believed that Tupac Inca Yupanqui built it. Vilcashuaman.

After the disappearance or dispersion of the Wari culture, other ethnic groups settled in the zone, same that did not reach the same sophisticated development level, but maintained a significant presence until the arrival of the Incas, who conquered and dominated them.

One of such groups was that of the Polcras, that settled in what is today Huamanga (Ayacucho), probably formed by Wari descendants. The other important group was that of the Chancas, who had long and ferocious encounters with the Incas (they surrounded Cusco in 1438) and were finally defeated by Pachacutec.

The policy the Incas applied to the kingdoms they conquered was to evict the local population, send it to zones controlled by their government, and repopulate them with people brought in from Cusco or its surroundings, totally faithful to the Inca. That is what they did in this place, and they also constructed buildings of the best Inca fabrication to serve as ceremonial and administrative centres, as well as military installations.

Low walls of the old Inca palace, of which there only remain the base and the niches. As can be seen, a Catholic church was built on top of it.

Trapezoidal Inca door.

Vilcashuaman (3000 m)

It is located 80 km south-east of Ayacucho and its name means "sacred falcon" (Huillcahuaman in the original Chanca language), which was a totemic animal of the Chancas and Pocras, that were the ones that built this sanctuary. Later on, the Incas built there an *Usnu* or ceremonial pyramid to worship the Sun, an Inca palace, military fortifications and other finely finished constructions.

Pachacutec started the construction of the temple, the palace, the ceremonial square and the army quarters for 30,000 men, while Huayna Capac completed the Aclla Wasi, the deposits and warehouses (more than 700) and additionally fortified the complex.

The importance of this complex rested on its superb location, because it controlled the interconnection roads between Cusco and Jauja (Central Peru) and the access roads to the coast (kingdom of Chincha and Pachacamac) and to the jungle (Huanta).

Over detailed ceramic art-craft piece representing a typical Andean church.

Santo Domingo church and convent (1548), with an unusual front, designed to celebrate mass outside the church.

Ayacucho possesses 38 churches constructed during the colonial period thanks to the donations made by rich *encomenderos* (foremen) and mine owners who settled in the zone, apart from the ones that the religious orders established in all new cities founded by the conquistadors.

Santa Teresa church and monastery (1703).

Ceramic figure of a popular character.

Sunday at the bullfights in the Santa Ana neighbourhood, with the church of the same name in the background.

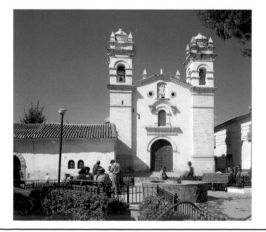

San Francisco de Paula Church (1713).

Ayacucho retable representing a hat shop, colourful sample of the popular mestizo art.

Reproduction of the church of Quinua and popular culture characters. Part of local tradition is to put these ceramic figures on the top of the roofs to keep evil away and attract good luck.

Flock of vicunas at Pampa Galeras, Ayacucho.

Elegantly attired alpaca, after participating in a community ceremony in the heights of Ayacucho.

Vicunas, South American members of the camel family, producer of the finest wool the Inca used to wear.

CENTRAL ANDES

Vast and rich valley formed by the Mantaro River.

Monument in the Anticona Mountain Pass (highest railroad point in the world) dedicated to the Polish engineer Ernest Malinowski, the builder of the railway that joins Lima with the centre of Peru.

The peasants have modified the slopes of the hills making small terraces adequate for growing their products.

The department of Junin is located east of Lima (Huancayo, the capital of the department is 300 km away), in central Peru, occupying an extensive zone of the central Andes and high jungle regions. This department has acquired universal fame because the highest railroad point in the world is located in the midst of its mountains: the Anticona Mountain Pass (4818 m), next to the snow-capped Ticlio mountain.

It is one of the most important development centres in the country, because of its high agricultural production and intense mining activity. The valley of the Mantaro River stands out in the Andes for its beauty and agricultural importance; it is full of small hamlets and peasant towns populated by descendants of one of the most hardened ethnic groups ever to inhabit the zone before the Incas: the Huancas.

Nevertheless, Junin's territory is mostly jungle, called jungle brow or high jungle (fluctuating between 600 and 2000 m.a.s.l.). This zone is very rich in the production of tea, coffee and fruit trees; besides, various native tribes or ethnic groups like the Ashaninka inhabit this land. The wealth of the zone is also made evident by its abundant flora and fauna, beautiful orchids, exuberant birds and colourful butterflies apart from its incredibly green natural landscapes, thick with vegetation and sprinkled with waterfalls and water springs.

Huancayo (3249 m) is the most important city of the zone. Because of its strategic location between the coast and the central jungle, surrounded by huge mining centres and fertile agricultural sierra valleys, it has developed fast, becoming one of the cities of higher commercial activity in Peru.

CENTRAL ANDES

Tarma countryside.

Artichoke field, very productive in the zone.

Numerous hamlets and small towns are scattered in valleys and ravines.

Palm leaf weavers create arrangements of different shapes. These will be used later during the celebrations of Palm Sunday.

Constitution Plaza and Huancayo Cathedral. Named Constitution because the unsuccessful Spanish constitution that granted some liberties to Indians and Creoles was signed there in 1812. The independence of Peru was also sworn in Huancayo on 20 November, 1820, and in 1854, Mariscal Ramon Castilla signed the abolition of slavery in the same city.

High relief engraving on Huamanga stone (Ayacucho) of a scene from Christ's Passion. Ocopa Convent.

Santa Rosa de Ocopa Convent (3360 m). The Franciscans established it in this region at the beginning of the XVIII century to send their evangelising missions to the jungle from there, (specially to evangelise the Ashaninka) and also to gather information and study its geography, flora, fauna and aborigine Amazon population.

The library of the Ocopa Convent is one of the largest existing in all Franciscan convents in Peru, with more than 20,000 volumes.

Tarma Cathedral dedicated to Santa Ana. The city of Tarma (3050 m), founded in 1538, is located in a warm valley, north of Huancayo.

Jungle land-scape near the city of San Ramon.

Top to bottom, butterflies of the species Morpho, Siproeta, Morpho and Heliconius.

Waterfalls located in San Ramon, small city in the province of Chanchamayo.

Exotic *baston de emperador* flower (Phoemeria magnificum).

HUARAZ

Late afternoon on the heights of snow-capped Huascaran, the highest mountain in Peru. Its southern peak is 6768 m, while the northern reaches 6655 m.

Huaraz is the capital of the department of Ancash (north of Lima), one of the few in Peru that consists of three geographic regions of great contrast: the desert coastal strip, the Andean snow-capped mountain and the high jungle of the Marañón River.

Huaraz (3027 m) has been destroyed many times by earthquakes (mainly the one of 31 May, 1970), reason why the city has not kept the typical Andean style of other towns in the region. Nevertheless, its main attraction is that

it has the highest and most beautiful snow-capped mountains in Peru, which have made of this city the mountain climbing capital of South America.

The socio-economic contrast of its population is a characteristic of the department of Ancash. The coast is industrialised thanks to its fishing and siderurgical activities, but this has drawn in thousands of Andean immigrants that have formed poverty belts around the cities, especially

in Chimbote. The mining activity in the sierra section of the department is very intense and productive, but as its operations are highly technological, it does not offer many employment opportunities. Agriculture is very rich thanks to the thawing of the snow from the mountains that provides water for the region all year round. Nevertheless, the prices paid for agricultural products are too low to cover the farmers' needs.

The last sun rays touch the peaks of Huandoy.

The Cordillera Blanca (White Mountain Range) owes its name to the snow that covers its mountains.

THE CORDILLERA BLANCA

It is 180 km long and formed by a series of 35 snow-capped mountains that rise above 6000 m, and by other lower peaks. Among its glaciated peaks there are Huascaran, Huandoy (6395 m), Alpamayo (5947 m), Huantsan (6395 m), Chopicalqui (6354 m), etc. It owes its name to the white glaciers that crown its peaks, contrasting with the mountain range that faces it, the Cordillera Negra (Black Mountain Range) characterised by the dark colour of the material of which it is formed. Both mountain ranges form a ravine crossed by the Santa River (draining into the coast) called Callejon de Huaylas.

Small, natural sparkling water fountain in the Huascaran National Park.

Paron Lagoon (4200 m.a.s.l.) located 32 km east of Caraz, the biggest in the Cordillera Blanca. There are 260 lagoons in the zone at altitude above 4000 m. In the background, partially covered, is the Piramide peak (5885 m).

Chacpá **flower** (Oreocallis Grandiflora) that only grows above 3000 meters.

Quenual (Polylepis sp.) grows above 4000 m. In the background, a lake at Llanganuco ravine (3800 m.a.s.l.). Huascaran National Park.

HUARAZ

Strong winds easily bend the *ichu*, gramineous plant that grows above 3500 m.a.s.l.

Puya Raimondi (bromeliácea) orchard in Huascaran National Park. Known by the native names of *titanca*, *ticatica*, *queshque* or *kunkush*. It reaches ten meters in height, lives an average of 50 years, with some of them reaching 100 years, and flowers only once, producing up to 8 million seeds and over three thousand flowers.

The people from the communities of the high-lands usually come down to the towns on Sunday. These two nice ladies do their shopping at the Caraz Sunday market.

Peasant women working in the field. Callejon de Huaylas.

Hamlet in the slopes of Huascaran.

Opposite page: Ranrahirca Square in the Callejon de Huaylas, at the foot of the Cordillera Blanca.

Hat shop. Caraz.

Chavin ceramic vessel with zoomorphic representation in its base.

CHAVIN CULTURE

This culture developed between 1200 BC and the first years of our era (it reached its peak between 1000 and 400 BC). Its centre of development was the ceremonial complex of Chavin de Huantar, located in the Callejon de Conchucos on the eastern basin of the White Mountain Chain (Cordillera Blanca), at 3180 m.a.s.l. Nevertheless, their cultural influence reached north up to the department of Lambayeque, including La Libertad, Cajamarca and Ancash; south to Lima, Ica, Ayacucho, Huancavelica and east to Huanuco. This influence is made evident by the Chavin style characteristics found in the cultural expressions of the local ethnic groups of these regions.

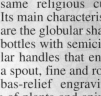

Chavin ceramic bottle with abstract design.

The essential aspect of this influence is based on religion, which was exported by Chavin in some way or another, be it by imposing their cults or by means of their religious iconographic characteristics that include feline designs, fangs, round scary eyes, serpent heads and human-like figures.

Chavin was a great and very prestigious ceremonial centre that priests and other inhabitants of the different ethnic groups belonging to a large territory used to frequent at regular intervals. Their religious activity derived into a vast cultural interchange where Chavin was the main culture and the others were recipients of its knowledge.

ARCHITECTURE

The Chavin ceremonial complex is composed of a series of pyramidal constructions, squares, stairways, underground chambers and passages, and monoliths engraved with religious iconography. Two temples used to form the complex: the Old Temple and the New Temple. The Old Temple was built at the end of the second millennium before Christ. It is shaped like a U, more than 100 meters wide and up to 16 meters tall. The façade of this building looks to the east (sunrise) and has only one entrance, precisely at this side.

Tello Obelisk.

The New Temple is located at the right side of the old one (south) and is bigger. It was built during the last Chavin period, between the years 500 and 200 BC. It is important to note that the old temple was neither destroyed, nor buried, but stood next to the new one, which was added to it. The walls of this temple used to be decorated with more than 40 protruding heads and numerous carved stone panels. The façade of the temple presents two finely carved columns and on top of them, a two-piece stone lintel, one of them white and the other black, meanig the duality of Chavin's religious world.

CERAMICS

Chavin ceramic art is scattered over a vast zone in the sierra and northern coast of Peru, absorbed by ethnic groups that must have shared the same religious cults. Its main characteristics are the globular shaped bottles with semicircular handles that end in a spout, fine and rough bas-relief engravings, figures of plants and animals (specially felines) and the stylised and abstract anthropomorphic creatures. The quality of the ceramic objects is very fine and thin, and their designs are precise and very delicate.

TELLO OBELISK

This is the most complex iconographic sculpture existing in Peru; it has not been possible to decipher it completely until now, although there are some approximate interpretations of it. It is almost three meters tall and was found in the circular plaza of the complex, buried 40 cm down.

Protruding head, the only one still holding its original position.

It is believed that the main figure of the obelisk is a dragon depicted in a masculine version on one side and a feminine one on the other (recognisable by the appendage both versions have under the abdomen: the masculine an ejaculating tree and the feminine an S).

Detail of column engraving at the entrance of the New Temple. The figure of a feline can be clearly seen at the far end, to the right.

Chavin de Huantar complex.

Columns and lintel at the entrance of the New Temple, called the Portico of the Falcons.

Subterraneous passage with protruding head.

Lanzon. This stone piece is engraved with stylised anthropomorphic and zoomorphic motifs.

TRUJILLO

This beautiful city has the same name as the place where Francisco Pizarro, conquistador of Peru, was born (he was born in Trujillo, Extremadura, Spain). Nonetheless, it was not Pizarro who founded it but his partner in the conquest, Diego de Almagro, on 6 December, 1534, and on the land granted for this purpose by the Chimor (Chimu) ruler, enemy of the Incas.

It was inhabited since its foundation by notable and noble conquistadors, and for this reason the City of Trujillo of New Castilla was granted the title of The Noblest City of Trujillo, by King Charles V, on 7 December, 1537.

Rich plantations were established around Trujillo during the colony, and the city could be developed thanks to their activity: agriculture. The rich land owners built beautiful leisure houses in the city. The style of the houses was characterised by the use of large porticos and huge interior patios, profusely decorated latticed windows and magnificent interior decoration.

Wrought iron window.

The Urquiaga House. The style is Neo-classic. It was from here that Trujillo proclaimed its independence from Spain in 1820

Trujillo's Main Square with the Cathedral (1610) in the background.

House with small colonial balcony.

Façade of typical colonial Trujillo house, with ample, decorated porticos.

TRUJILLO

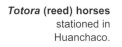

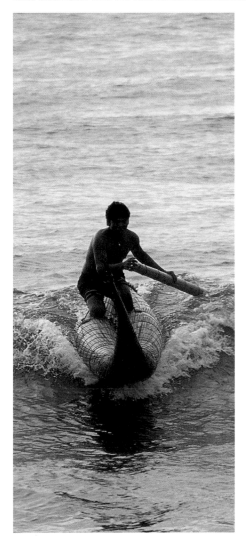

Late afternoon over the Huanchaco resort and its old pier.

Totora (reed) horses stationed in Huanchaco.

Local fishermen, as did their ancestors from the kingdoms of Moche and Chimor, go out on these small *totora* reed rafts, called *totora* horses to earn their daily income.

The sun sets over Huanchanco, a propitious time to go out fishing.

Chimu Culture

Dog figure.

About the year 800 AD and after the dominion of the Wari kingdom started weakening, a new local kingdom began to consolidate in the northern Peruvian coast. This nation settled in the same zone where others before them had reached an ample cultural development (Moche, Lambayeque) and almost at the same time when in Cusco, the Incas were taking form, to afterwards, towards the XV century, encounter each other with the resulting disappearance of the Chimor Kingdom, or Chimu culture.

The Chimor extended through the northern coast of Peru from the valley of the Chillon River, north of Lima, to Tumbes, in the Ecuadorian border. Its founder, as per the information gathered by the chroniclers of the conquest, was a personality by the name of Tacaynamo, who also started building the monumental complex of Chan Chan and a series of roads that connected his kingdom from north to south and from the coast to the Andean valleys, controlling the administrative centres of the kingdom. After him came Gucricaur, Nancen-Pinco (who is attributed a further expansion of the kingdom) and Minchancaman, who was defeated by the Incas during the wars between the years 1462 and 1470. The Incas took this last Chimor emperor to Cusco and married him to an Inca princess.

Chimu bottle representing a bicephalous bird.

Ceramic spondyllus shell.

This was a society based on religious worshipping, as were all others at the time, meaning the existence of a theocratic pattern where the king or the maximum governor was of mythological origin and his presence was considered divine. The level beneath the king had very intrinsic divisions in accordance with the function of each person (hereditary positions). The administrators of the conquered nations had a great deal of power to govern the subjects, collect taxes and control the production of the land.

This culture developed a sophisticated agriculture with extensive irrigation channels, large capacity water reservoirs, agricultural tools and soil treatment that allowed for two to three harvests a year in many valleys with not very fertile soil. The type of farming and subsequent storage of the production was made under state planning, so that difficult periods could be anticipated, as draughts or floods caused by El Niño phenomenon.

Metallurgy

They mastered metals, specially gold, silver and copper, as well as diverse alloys specialising in gold-plated and silver-plated metal pieces. The governors of this culture used to wear gold-plated or silver-plated copper vests (*uncu*) as well as gold and silver necklaces, ear ornaments and masks.

Ceramics

The Chimu or Chimor inherited their skillfulness in ceramics from their ancestors, the Moche, although they did not reach the same level of quality. They assimilated the influence of cultures like the Wari and the styles of Cajamarca and Recuay. The great difference between Moche and Chimu ceramics is that the first mentioned shaped the pieces by hand, while the latter generalised the use of moulds.

Chimu ceramic objects are extremely polished and use mainly dark colours. They tend to represent objects like plants, animals, fruits, people and mythological beings, using the bas-relief and trowelling techniques. After the Inca conquest, they took in as a characteristic touch, to put a little monkey on one of the handles of their ceramic pieces.

Navigators

The Chimu were great navigators, as are today the people of the coast they used to inhabited, and as the myth about the arrival of the founder of their kingdom suggests. They employed the typical *totora* reed horses to catch fish and molluscs close to the beach. But for longer trips, they developed a kind of raft made of trunks tied together with one or two masts and cloth sails (the ones found are square and triangular), driven by wooden oars and a system of mobile trunks placed on the stern and the prow of the vessel, that ensured great stability at sea.

Chimu vessel showing a character identified with the god of corn.

Bottle shaped as an *aryballo* with bas-relief decorations belonging to the Chimu-Inca period.

Bird figure representation of the Chimu-Inca period.

Central sector of the Chan Chan citadel. It was the capital of the Chimor (Chimu) kingdom and had an extension of about 24 km². It consisted of ten major complexes, each of them with its own palaces, dwelling places, water reservoirs, food storehouses, ceremonial square, streets, passages, access ramps and funeral chambers.

Entrance to one of the main Chan Chan squares. The walls are decorated with patterns of marine birds and fish.

Frieze with a representation of the decapitator, apparently, the god of water. This figure is next to others in what it is believed was a patio where human sacrifices were performed. Huaca de la Luna, Moche Culture.

Huaca del Sol (Huaca of the Sun). Monumental pyramid with only one fourth of its original construction remaining, since the Spaniards and the floods of the Moche River destroyed it. Moche culture.

Huaca de la Luna (Huaca of the Moon), facing the colossal Huaca del Sol. They formed the capital of the Mochica Kingdom.

Beautiful and not very well known murals in the Huaca El Brujo (the wizard) in Trujillo, Moche culture. The image of the decapitator with two trophy heads hanging from his hands can be appreciated.

Huaca Arco Iris (rainbow), located close to Chan Chan. Chimu culture.

Polychrome, high-relief representation of an important Moche character.

CHICLAYO

Chiclayo Cathedral.

Iguana (Iguana iguana) in the woods of the Batan Grande National Reserve.

Chiclayo, the capital of the department of Lambayeque (760 km north of Lima), is located on the arid Peruvian coastal strip. This place has recently captured the interest of the scientific community of the world as a result of the finding of tombs belonging to lords of important pre-Inca cultures: the Royal Tombs of the Lord of Sipan and the Tombs of Batan Grande, or Sican.

These tombs and other additional findings, have unveiled an impressive amount of gold and silver ornaments, handcrafted by Peruvians of ancient times. These valuable, historical jewels are being exhibited in three of the best museums in Peru, and all three are located in the department of Lambayeque: the Bruning Museum (Lambayeque culture), the Royal Tombs of Sipan Museum (Moche culture) - both in the town of Lambayeque (10 minutes away from Chiclayo) - and the Sican Museum (Lambayeque culture), in the neighbouring town of Ferreñafe.

Apart from this, the Batan Grande Pyramids (Sican) and the architectonic complex of Túcume (Lambayeque and Chimu cultures) are also located in this area, with 26 gigantic pyramids, standing out the 700 m long, 270 m wide, and 30 m high Huaca Larga pyramid.

Millenarian carob tree at Batan Grande National Reserve.

The Túcume Pyramids, Sican or Lambayeque culture centre.

MOCHE CULTURE

Towards the first years of the Christian era, diverse ethnic groups and highly populated societies that had marked differences in their cultural development inhabited the northern coast of Peru. This over population generated a scarcity of resources as also warlike confrontations, even with groups coming from the Andes. For this reason, the inhabitants started organising themselves and uniting around a military powerful group that had best developed its agricultural techniques.

This is how the Moche Culture (100 - 800 AD) started and became established in the coast of the departments of La Libertad (Trujillo), Lambayeque, Piura, and according to some archaeological evidence, also Chota, Cajamarca (Northern Andes). Its capital was located in the valley of Moche where the pyramids known as Huaca del Sol and Huaca de la Luna (Huacas of the Sun and of the Moon) had been constructed.

The main characteristics of this culture are the high level of cultural and artistic production it reached, as also its monumental architecture. The planned agriculture it developed was capable of feeding a vast population using irrigation channels, water reservoirs and food storage. It also established a system of taxes and a social structure strictly based on hierarchy, but efficient in controlling power. Nevertheless, as could be determined through the study of the archaeological findings, it was a society of great contrasts, with a very rich elite and a great mass of poor and subjugated people.

Its vertical political organisation was based on religion and the belief that its leaders were divine beings. For that reason, they adorned themselves profusely with exquisite gold and silver jewels, as could be confirmed at the time the almost intact tomb of the Lord of Sipan, one of the Moche governors in Lambayeque, was found.

CERAMICS

Moche ceramic work is the most beautiful of all American pre-Columbian cultures, especially for the perfection achieved in figurative representation of objects and subjects. For instance, they portrayed the faces of their kings, priests and personalities of their society; depicted sick people and gave account of the sicknesses affecting them with almost photographic skill. Sadness, happiness, war, love, sex, religion and death were also beautifully represented.

They employed diverse techniques, as individual moulding of the pieces as well as mass production using moulds (bottles, vessels and other functional pieces,for example). Their main characteristic is the stirrup-shape handles and the globular shape of the ceramics.

METALLURGY

They mastered gold, silver, copper and other metals with which they made beautiful pieces, employing casting, hammering, repoussage and welding. Gold, the most precious metal, was reserved for religious, politic and military leaders, be it when alive or for funeral ornamentation.

They used gold and silver to make ear adornments, crowns, ceremonial vessels, figures of men, animals, and anthropomorphic animals with divine qualities, breastplates and necklaces among others. Gold was associated with the sun and masculinity, while silver was associated with the moon and femininity.

Bottle representing a Moche character wearing a feline-shaped headpiece and large ear ornaments, a symbol of power.

Ceramic bottle representing an important Moche character, as clearly shown by the decorated headpiece and ear ornaments.

Erotic Moche ceramic.

Moche ceramic vase-portrait depicting skilfully the weeping and sadness.

Erotic Moche ceramic. Man with an expression of delight.

Ceramic vase-portrait depicting an obese character with an undefined facial expression.

Moche bottle with an interesting representation of a condor devouring a human leg.

LAMBAYEQUE CULTURE (700 AD - 1350 AD)

This culture settled in the department of Lambayeque (700 AD - 1350 AD), inside the Batan Grande National Reserve, is also called by some scholars the Sican culture, for the name of the place its nucleus was located. It originated as a result of the decadence of the Moche culture and the direct influence of the Wari and Cajamarca cultures, and started falling down with the attacks of the Chimu culture that finally absorbed it. This may be the reason why for a long time, there appeared to be no differences between them, but today, archaeologists have come across sufficient evidence to determine there were two different cultures concerned. Its area of influence extended barely outside the present department of Lambayeque (it reached the south of Piura and Chicama, in Trujillo), and concentrated in the valleys of the La Leche and Chancay Rivers; nevertheless it produced exquisite metallurgic works of art.

In the same way as its neighbours in time and space, the economy of the

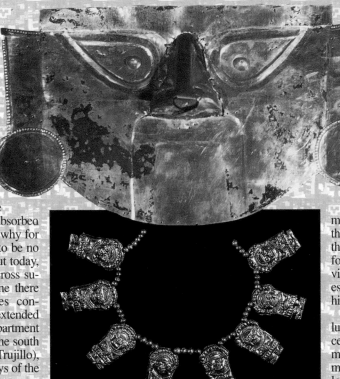

Lambayeque golden necklace with the representations of Naylamp.

Lambayeque golden funerary mask depicting a face of the lord of winged eyes or Naylamp.

Lambayeque society was based on a successfully developed agriculture, backed by its vertical theocratic state, with members of the dominant class having family bonds through alliances with those from the other valleys.

The Spanish chroniclers managed to gather information about the myth regarding the foundation of this culture, according to which its founder, Naylamp, arrived to this land via the sea from very far away and established himself in the valley with his women, servants and soldiers.

Among its most important metallurgic work are the famous *tumi* or ceremonial knives and its funeral masks. The *tumi* bears the face of the maximum deity of Lambayeque, the lord of the winged eyes, or Naylamp (also appearing on vessels and other objects), identifiable by the lines of the eyes that go up at the end, the prominent nose and pointy ears.

THE LORD OF SIPAN

On 26 July, 1987, close to the small village of Sipan (40 km SE of Chiclayo, in the Pomalca Cooperative), the most important discovery in Peruvian archaeology of the twentieth century took place: The Royal Tombs of the Lord of Sipan were found. The discovery is given this degree of importance because, the tombs were found almost intact, something that has happened very seldom as since the arrival of the Spanish conquistadors, it was common practice to profane them in order to steal important gold and silver pieces, as well as ceramics and textiles.

The complex, called Huaca Rajada, consists of two adobe pyramids separated

Tomb of the Lord of Sipan, the lord of the Moche culture.

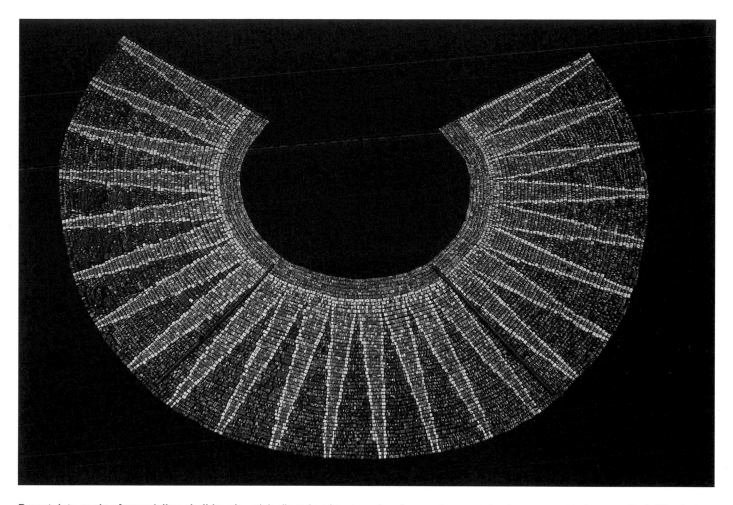

Breastplate made of spondyllus shell beads, originally red and cream colour (green at present due to copper oxide impregnation). The design shows 24 red rays coming out from the centre of the breastplate, symbolically associated with the solar cult of the Lord of Sipan.

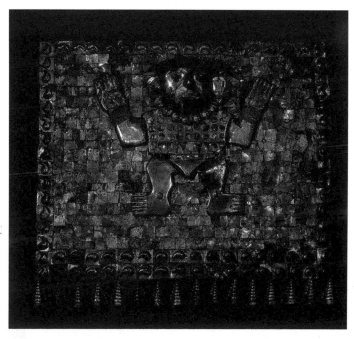

Square standard. Made of pieces of golden copper that were sewed to a cloth. There is a human figure in the centre with Moche ornamentation such as a necklace with owl heads around its neck, a head-piece, turquoise bracelets on its wrists, as well as other pieces of jewellery on its body. It is a deity surrounded by representations of a fruit called *ulluchu*, reason why it is known as the ulluchu deity.

by a huge square. It must have been a religious funeral complex used by several generations of the Moche hierarchy, which finding has given local scholars new and deeper evidence regarding the life and customs of the Moche culture.

For example, it is now known that the Lord of Sipan died at 45 years of age, that he was 1.66 m tall and was born approximately the year 300 AD. He was found inside a wooden coffin, lying down, with his feet pointing north and his head south, sumptuously dressed: silver sandals, gold ear ornaments with turquoise incrustations, a golden crown, gold and silver necklaces and many other dress pieces, also of gold, silver and copper.

He was buried with another eight persons: three young women, two men and a boy at his side, and there were two more men in the top part of his tomb. The skeletons of two llamas and a dog were also found in the tomb.

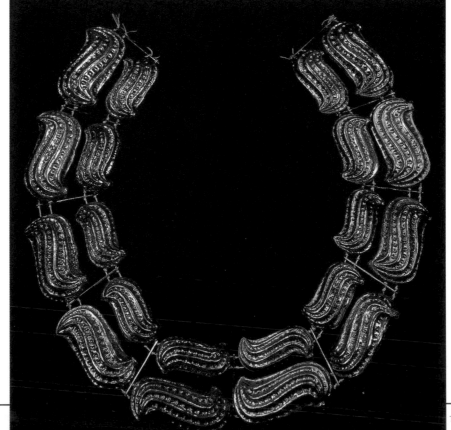

Open arms figure, made of golden copper. It has a representation of the deity of the ulluchus in the centre, same as in the standards.

Gold and silver necklace. Representing the fruit of the peanut plant found at the feet of the Lord of Sipan.

CHICLAYO

THE OLD LORD OF SIPAN

After the finding of the Lord of Sipan, another burial was found in the first part of the funeral complex with ornaments as sumptuous as the previous one, that made the scholars assume a Moche dignitary, several generations older than the Lord of Sipan, was concerned. The pieces found in the burial are of a more complex religious character than the other one, what led to assume that at the time of this Old Lord of Sipan, politic and religious functions were more amalgamated.

Copper effigy representing the "Ai-Apaec" deity. It was found as part of a headpiece in the tomb of the Old Lord of Sipan.

Rattler made on a repoussage silver sheet representing the Moche god "Ai-Apaec" or decapitator. The Old Lord of Sipan.

THE PRIEST

The tomb of this important personality of the Moche society was found south-east of the funeral platform and the burial corresponds to the same period as the Lord of Sipan. This priest was about 40 years of age and 1.60 m tall. The ornaments found with him are basically of religious use, as the crown with an owl with open wings and the sacrificial cup, or the nine-piece necklace related to the cult of the moon and its cycles.

Golden copper necklace decorated with representations of nine smiling human heads, found in the tomb of the Priest. The teeth on the heads were made with shell incrustations.

THE NORTH COAST

The sun sets over the Talara sea and its oil wells.

A fisherman of prawn larvae coming out from the tepid waters of the Piura sea.

A fisherman holding the rare mirror fish, as this species is called in Mancora (Selene peruvianus).

The beaches of Mancora, in the northern department of Piura. The climate there is warm all year round because of its proximity to the Equator. The fishermen have left their fishing gear on the beach.

THE NORTH COAST

Typical house of the northern farmers. The tree in front of the house offers vital shade and coolness in the summer, when temperatures rise above 30 degrees centigrade.

Palm tree field in Sullana, Piura. Its warm climate and abundance of water makes it a very favourable zone for agriculture in Peru.

White heron (Casmerodius albus egretta) in a rice field. Sullana.

It's very common to see northern farmers using donkeys for transport and as beasts of burden.

Short-tailed field-tyrant (Muscigralla bre-vicauda), bird that abounds in the northern Peruvian coast.

Beautiful Vermilion flycatcher (Pyrocephalus rubinus obscurus). The male of this species is red and black (on the picture), while the female is brownish.

Ferruginous pygmy-owl or *paca-paca* (Glaucidium b. brasilianum) that lives in the wooded areas of the region.

Small, long-tailed lizard (Tropidurus sp.) begins to camouflage coming out of its hole.

Dark-billed cuckoo (Coccyzus melacoryphus) with its unmistakable dark band at the level of the eye.

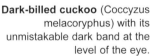

Carob trees (Prosopis spp.) on the fields of Piura.

The Sechura Desert, one of the driest in the world (50 km south of Piura).

The wind forms these small mounds on the sand, in Sechura.

MANGROVE SWAMPS

The Tumbes mangrove swamps form a barrier against the erosion.

Small Tumbes crocodile (Crocodylus acutus), raised in captivity to avoid its extinction.

Blue heron (Florida caerulea), an inhabitant of the mangrove swamps.

MANGROVE SWAMPS

Stylish flight of a stilt (Himantopus himantopus mexicanus).

Magnificent frigatebird (Fregata magnificens). The male bird has a black head and red breast that is inflated to attract the female. The female has a white head and neck.

A flock of stilts. They abound at the edge of the swamps.

Frigatebird flying to its nest at sunset.

The National Sanctuary "Mangrove Swamps of Tumbes" is located in the delta formed by the Tumbes River when entering the sea, near the border with Ecuador. These are the only mangrove swamps in Peru and the types of mangrove that grow in its salty waters are: the red mangrove (Rhizophora mangle), the salty mangrove (Avicennia germinans), the white mangrove (Laguncularia racemosa) and the button mangrove (Conocarpus erectus).

In the area live numerous species of crustaceans, molluscs, fish, birds, iguanas, the Tumbes crocodile, the *tamandua* (small anteater) and other species .

CAJAMARCA

Belen Church with its unfinished towers (they were not finished for the purpose of receiving the subvention for incomplete churches). Its construction lasted from second half of the XVII century to 1744

Old cattle hacienda of La Colpa.

Cumbemayo Canal (1000 years BC) more than 9 km long, located on the Cumbe mountain (3600 m).

Cajamarca

Everybody participates in carnival, parading or throwing water at whoever happens to pass by.

Cajamarca peasant women.

Little windows of Otuzco. These are niches carved on the rocks, used by the Cajamarca people (Cajamarca culture 1100 BC - 50 BC) to bury their dead.

The most important date associated with Cajamarca is 16 November, 1532, when the conquistador Pizarro, imprisoned Inca Atahualpa, signifying the end of the Inca nation and the beginning of the Spanish conquest. Atahualpa was executed in the same city after having given the Spaniards a valuable ransom for his freedom.

The city is located on an extensive Andean valley (2750 m) in the department of the same name, north of Lima (850 km) and is one of the Peruvian cities that shows more Spanish characteristics, since the Spanish troops going out to conquer the Tahuantisuyu, concentrated there.

Cajamarca carnival. A mixture of Andean tradition and modernity.

Wild flower of the Cajamarca fields.

KUELAP

Kuelap archaeological complex. It used to be a walled in city where a select group of inhabitants of the Chachapoya kingdom resided.

The fascinating archaeological complex of Kuelap is located near the city of Chachapoyas (founded in 1538), capital of the department of Amazonas (Peruvian Northeast, border with Ecuador). It is a walled in city built by the Chachapoya. Its construction started in the VII century of our era and continued up to the Inca period and the Spanish colonisation (XVI century).

The Chachapoya were a nation that developed in what is now department of Amazonas (were its core used to be), but extended to Ucayali and parts of Piura and La Libertad departments. It covered the regions of the high nor oriental jungle or Amazon Andes, geographic

Narrow Kuelap entrance door: only one person can enter it at a time. The wall is almost 20 meters high.

The ruins of a circular construction lay in the north sector of the second platform. The whole east side of the complex can be observed from there.

boundary of the sierra formed by an Andes mountain chain and the Amazon basin, in the midst of a vast zone of tropical rain forests.

The Incas conquered the kingdom of the Chachapoya around the middle of the XV century, led by Tupac Inca Yupanqui, and subsequently Inca Huayna Capac consolidated the Inca domination in the zone. Nevertheless, when the Spaniards arrived, the Chachapoya became their allies and the conquistadors recruited many of them to fight against the Incas.

The Kuelap complex (3040 m.a.s.l.) was built along several periods of the development of the Chachapoya kingdom

Chachapoya house in Kuelap reconstructed in accordance with existing archaeological evidence.

Ruins of a Chachapoya circular house in Kuelap. Its walls reach a height of 4 m.

and after the Inca conquest and first years of the colony it became abandoned and decadent. Its construction is monumental and majestic; its walls are almost 20 m high and its more than 500 m long.

The fortress, as this complex is usually called, has three levels or platforms over which diverse edifications were built, most of them as dwelling places for the inhabitants. The main characteristic of these dwelling places is their circular shape and the external high relief decoration of the walls.

Spectacular Amazon ceramic sarcophagi, 2 m high each, located in Karajía, near the town of Luya in Amazonas. Each sarcophagus contains a mummy wrapped in funeral covers together with ceramic objects and other crafts. Access to them is very difficult since they are placed at the edge of a precipice, 200 m from the ground. Chachapoya Culture.

Above and left:
Parts of the walls of Chachapoya houses with external deco-rations. The most common motifs are simple, double and triple rhombus and broken lines.

Opposite page:
Of the 30,000 varieties of orchids existing in the world, 3,000 grow in Chachapoyas.

AMAZON JUNGLE

Amazon River. If its extension is measured taking into account the Ucayali River, one of its principal tributaries in Peru, the Amazon River would be 6762 km long, therefore the largest river in the world.

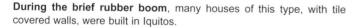
During the brief rubber boom, many houses of this type, with tile covered walls, were built in Iquitos.

Iron House (1887) designed by Gustave Eiffel at the request of the eccentric millionaire of Bolivian origin, Baca Díaz.

Also known as low jungle or *omagua*, the Amazon region is the vast plain that lies east of the Andes mountain range which altitude, with respect to the sea, fluctuates between 80 and 400 m. It is full of rivers, lagoons, swamps and meanders and is the habitat of the largest assortment of flora and fauna species found in one and the same place in the planet, and is also the oxygen reserves or lungs of Earth.

The Amazon region houses at least 65 native ethnic groups that have coexisted for many years with their environment in an equilibrated way. They have preserved their customs and their own tongues up to now, in spite of the growing occidentalisation of the jungle, where huge economic interests exploit their resources as was the case in the past with rubber and keeps on going today with timber, gold and plants used by the pharmaceutical industry.

The most emblematic river of the jungle is the Amazon River, discovered by the Spanish conquistador Francisco de Orellana on 12 February, 1542. It is the river with the highest volume of water in the world, reaching an average of 100,000 m^3 per second; its width is 5 km in its widest part and its deeper zone is 240 m. It varies in length according to the starting point being considered, but it is approximately 6500 km long.

Passenger and cargo vessels, typical of jungle rivers, moor along the banks of the Momón River, a tributary of the Amazon River.

Iquitos Cathedral.

IQUITOS

Iquitos is the largest city in the Peruvian jungle (over 400,000 inhabitants) and its name comes from the Amazon tribe of the Iquitos. In 1729, the Jesuit missionary Pablo Maroni founded the mission of the Itaya River for the purpose of evangelising the tribes of the Yameos and Iquitos. In 1739, ten years later, another mission by the name of Santa Barbara de Nanay (on the river of the same name) was created, and this induced many of the inhabitants to settle around both missions. The town of San Pablo de los Napeanos, that originated what is today the city of Iquitos, was founded in 1757.

Iquitos reached its highest peak of prosperity at the end of the XIX and beginning of the XX century, when the vulcanisation of rubber used in wheels for carriages, became popular. More than twenty companies, dedicated to the exportation of this product obtained from the rubber tree or *shiringa*, opened for business in Iquitos. For this purpose, they used the labour of native communities exploiting and enslaving the natives to extract the rubber from the trees. The real peak lasted merely twenty years, between 1899 and 1910 to later enter a period of decadence and further shut down, due to the success obtained by the English and the Dutch in their efforts to acclimatise rubber plants grown in the Amazon region and produce rubber in their Asian colonies.

Riverside houses in Iquitos.

Sunset at the Morona Lagoon (Moronacocha) in Iquitos.

Floating houses in the district of Belén, on the confluence of the rivers Amazon and Itaya.

Banana sale at the Belén market, Iquitos.

Vessel called peque-peque (for the sound its motor makes) transporting bags of charcoal elaborated deep in the jungle. Momón River, tributary of the Amazon.

Amazon fish wrapped in banana (*bijao*) leafs and grilled, is one of the most popular typical dishes of the region.

Wharf at Padre Isla (Padrecocha), in front of Iquitos.

Family of Bora natives, established in the zone north of Iquitos.

Curaca (local governor) Yagua communicating through the *maguaré*, an instrument for conveying sounds made of a hollow trunk which is banged with some mallets and which sound travels a distance of 30 km.

Yagua tribe natives, they speak Peba-yagua and their original name was Nihamwo. They live in small disperse groups of two or three families and usually work with the settlers cutting wood in the jungle.

Beautiful heliconia flower (Heliconia sp.)

The department of Loreto, to which Iquitos belongs, houses 24 tribes or native ethnic groups, that have dealings with the occidentilised towns of the Amazon jungle. The inhabitants of these ethnic groups and their descendants are now estimated in more than 100,000; nevertheless, there are other groups (around 20) which population keeps apart from the rest of the country. Their exact number is not known, but it is estimated that they could amount to five or eight thousand individuals.

The Aguaruna, Bora, Capanagua, Chamicuro, Huambisa, Piro, Secoya, Shipibo-Conibo, Ticuna and Yagua are among the best known ethnic groups. Each of them still maintains its customs, tribal organisation, dress, and tongue, and most are friendly with the settlers and foreigners that visit them; nevertheless violent conflicts can originate when they feel their territory is being invaded by settlers looking to exploit wood or expand their agricultural fields. In fact, the occidentalisation and the unstoppable depredation of the jungle are an ever-growing menace to the preservation of these native ethnic groups that can do little against the progress of "civilisation".

Canoes are the main means of transport.

During the dry season, between April and November when it does not rain, these little *cochas* or lagoons will dry completely.

Woman from a family of settlers lays down her laundry to dry. In the background, small lagoons or *cochas* formed by the Nanay River.

Victoria Regia, the largest aquatic lily in the world.

Huimba **or cotton tree** (Ceiba samauma) is the local name of this giant tree of more than 8 meters in diameter (around its thickest point) and 50 meters tall.

Local wild animal tamer caught this little tiger cat (Leopardus pardalis).

Anaconda (Eunectes murinus) can reach a length of ten meters and weigh 250 kilos.

White caiman (Caiman crocodiles) holding a piranha in its mouth.

MANU

Sloth, a very slow moving mammal, travels from branch to branch holding himself up with his long, claw-shaped nails. Its metabolism is very slow, and so are his movements. He feeds on leaves and flowers. There are two types of these mammals in the Manu and the whole Amazon jungle, the two-toed one (Choloepus hoffmanni) and the three-toed one (Bradypus variegatus).

The Manu National Park is located in the department of Madre de Dios and is considered by UNESCO as a Biosphere Reserve and Cultural Patrimony of Humanity. It extends from the eastern basin of the Andes mountain chain of the department of Cusco to the low plains of Madre de Dios, covering 1,881,200 hectares, of which one million five hundred thousand are intangible area, 257 thousand cover the muffler zone (the controlled presence of scholars and tourists is permitted) and 90 thousand are of multiple use.

The Manu covers high Andean zones or *puna*, the very damp mountain rain-forest (jungle brow), the subtropical rain-forest (high and low jungle) and the tropical rainforest. The park shelters more than 300 species of trees, 925 species of birds, 1300 species of butterflies and 200 species of mammals.

Fruits of the orleans baum plant (Bixa orellana), which seeds are employed as a natural colouring agent for food and cosmetics. The natives use it to paint their face and hair.

Bromelia, epifit plant that lives on tree trunks and branches.

Yellow-tailed woolly monkey (Lagothrix flavicauda).

Humboldt's woolly monkey (Lagothrix lagotricha).

Maquisapa or spider monkey (Ateles paniscus), that lives in the virgin forest of Madre de Dios.

Small blue headed parrot (Pionus menstruus).

Beautiful couple of macaws: blue and yellow (Ara ararauna) and scarlet (Ara macao).

Mealy Amazon parrot (Amazona farinosa).

Cuvier's toucan (Ramphastus cuvieri).

Yellow spotted Amazon River turtle or *taricaya* (Podocnemis unifilis) a variety of jungle turtle.

Little South American river turtle or *charapa* (Podocnemis expansa).

Mata mata (Chelys fimbriata) aquatic turtle.

Andean cock-of-the-rock (Rupicola peruviana).

Situlli **flower** (Heliconia sp.).

Trees like the ceticos (Cecropia sp.), balsa (Ochroma sp.) cedar (Cedrela sp.), *tornillo* (Cedrelinga catenaeformis) and rubber tree (Hevea brasiliensis) among others are characteristic of the Manu jungle.

Puma (Puma concolor) an inhabitant of the high and low jungle.

INDEX